Show Your Tongue

Other books by Günter Grass

The Tin Drum
Cat and Mouse
Dog Years
The Plebeians Rehearse the Uprising
Four Plays
Speak Out!
Local Anaesthetic
Max: A Play
From the Diary of a Snail
Inmarypraise
In the Egg and Other Poems
The Flounder
The Meeting at Telgte
Headbirths
Drawings and Words 1954–1977
On Writing and Politics 1967–1983
Etchings and Words 1972–1982
The Rat

Günter Grass

Show Your Tongue

TRANSLATED BY JOHN E. WOODS

A Helen and Kurt Wolff Book

Harcourt Brace Jovanovich, Publishers

San Diego   New York   London

Copyright © 1988 by Luchterhand Literaturverlag GmbH, Darmstadt
English translation copyright © 1989 by Harcourt Brace Jovanovich, Inc.

Library of Congress Cataloging-in-Publication Data

Grass, Günter, 1927–
[Zunge zeigen. English]
Show your tongue / Günter Grass ; translated by John E. Woods.—
1st ed.
p. cm.
Translation of: Zunge zeigen.
"A Helen and Kurt Wolff book."
ISBN 0-15-182090-2 — ISBN 0-15-682330-6 (pbk.)
1. Grass, Günter, 1927–   —Journeys—India. 2. Authors,
German—20th century—Biography. 3. India—Description and
travel—1981– I. Title.
PT2613.R338Z47713   1989
838′.91403—dc19
[B]   88-27116

Printed in the United States of America

First United States edition

A B C D E

For Mr. and Mrs. Karlekar
and the Calcutta Social Project

GRASS
87

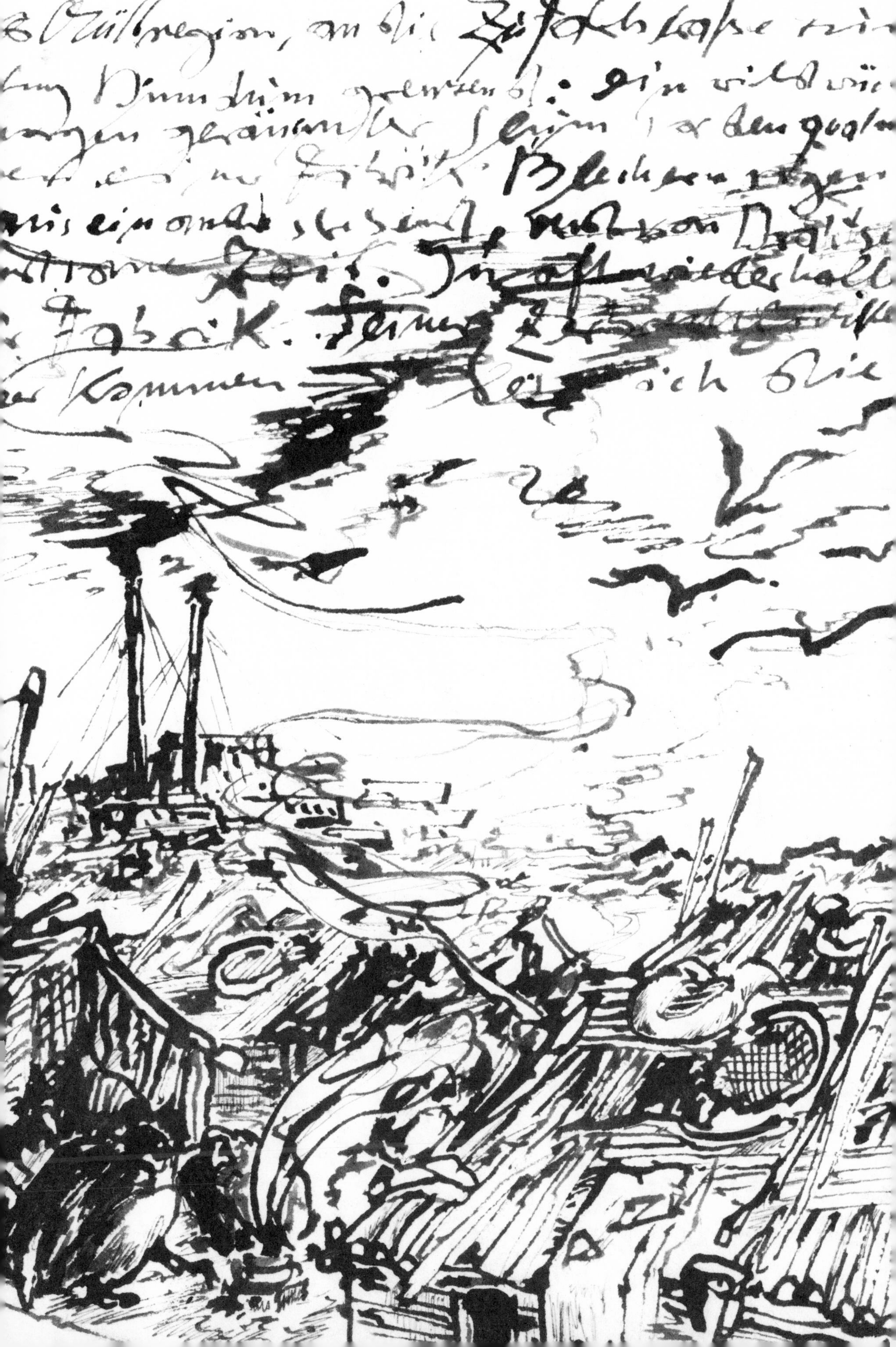

Auf dem
Hongkong Bank
eine Mau
Das Un
glatt
niemand sieht
Schablone

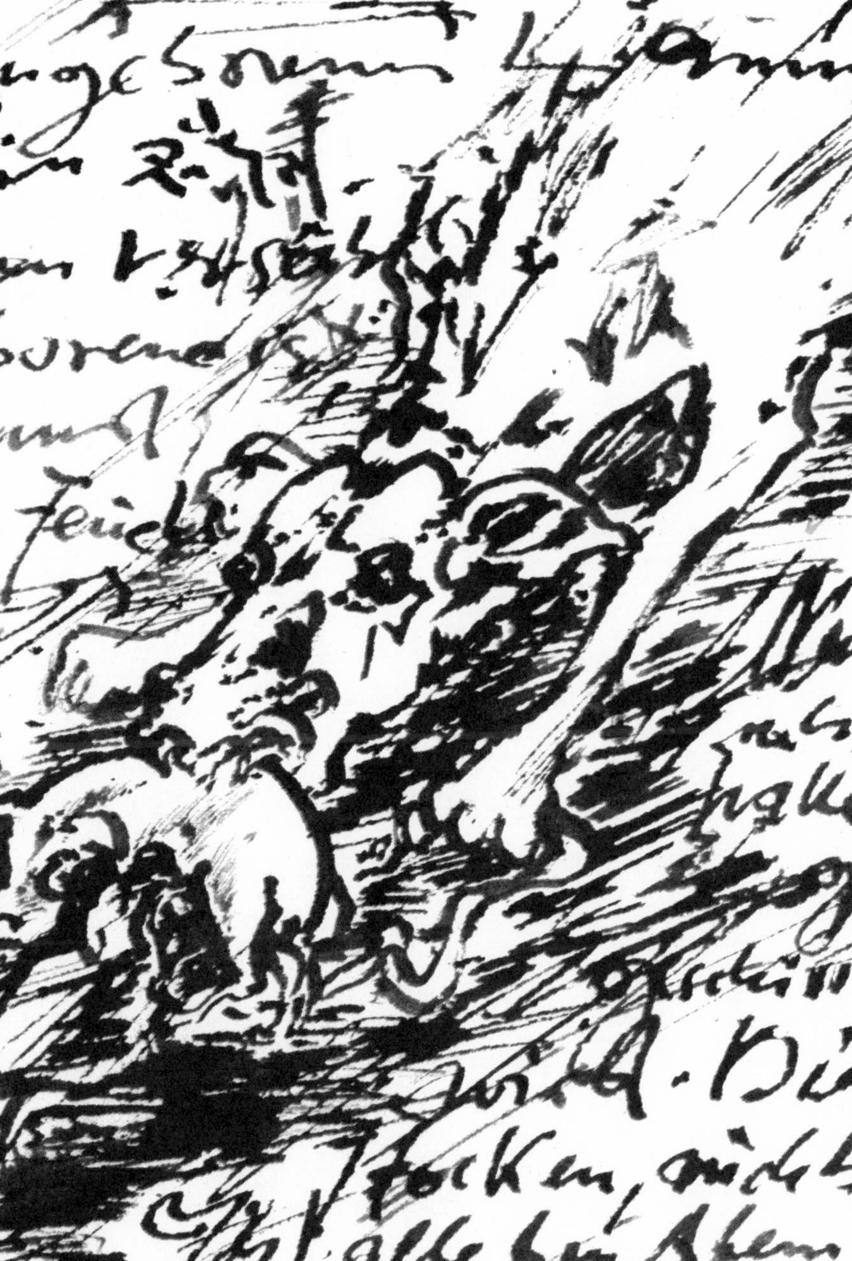

On the North Side of Calcutta

a rider, all in bronze on a horse too small for him, his head too large under his military cap, massively bespectacled yet raising an imperiously directing hand—To Delhi! To Delhi!—though never budging, since as a monument plus pedestal he is rooted to one place, a circle-intersection of five streets called, appropriately, Five Point Crossing, a rider, then, Subhas Chandra Bose by name, a.k.a. Netaji, the Revered Leader.

When I first encountered him, eleven years ago, as a cavalry man, or reduced to a bust, or drawn up to full height (but always, whether in stone or cast metal, wearing his glasses), I had only vague notions about him and his global significance. From the newsreels of my school days—he came on the scene, I think, before Stalingrad, or shortly thereafter—I recalled the name and the way Bose, in civvies, inspected his Indian Legion decked out in Wehrmacht uniforms, and how he shook hands with Himmler, with Hitler, on our flickering neighborhood screen—just as I will see him, forty-five years later, in photos in Calcutta's Victoria Memorial Museum, in uniform, side by side with Japanese generals, drinking wine with Yamamoto, an acquaintance from Berlin days.

Netaji, the unsuccessful hero, dubbed "The Springing Tiger." Gandhi's stout adversary. Stirring orator before the world's microphones. Subhas Chandra Bose, whose legend has remained the stuff of Bengali dreams. On a white horse he will ride into the city along the Hooghly River, tomorrow, soon, someday, from the north perhaps, where at Five Point Crossing he will salute himself, on a horse too small for him, his head too large, yet cast for all time in bronze, hand to his cap.

Our steamer trunk arrived before we did. After a long train ride (three days now in Calcutta), this is our second trip from

1

Baruipur to Ballygunge Station. We're living in a summer house south of the city. Like flotsam, thrown in with everything and everybody, skin rubbing skin, sweat mixing with sweat. But we remain aliens wherever we are, regardless of the palpating stares all around. Distance and nearness lose meaning.

Dozing inside the tin box. At the six or seven stops along the way, people get off and climb aboard at the same time; each time, a brief soundless struggle. After the fourth station, the city begins, villages merge into slums. Even along the embankment, a border of slums; behind them, newly constructed ruins. Above us, handstraps, each overloaded. None of the fans is turning. The windows are open, but the draft can't make it to the middle of the car. Another lurch, and with it, above our heads, the shifting of burlap bags full of green coconuts, baskets of bananas, rag bundles laced up in cord, chickens in cages.

Each car is a ruin. Seats missing, frames out of kilter, obstructing iron rods. The remaining lightbulbs, protected by wire mesh, dangle wildly from their entrails. Everything sticky, the floor slimy with the red snot of betel juice. Clusters of young boys, tangled, plug the permanently open car doors. To them belongs the moving air.

On these commuter trains, Indian society (for the duration of the trip) is casteless. Even in the cars reserved for women, they sit, they stand penned together, rubbing against one another, sharing handstraps in polyfingered confusion. Emaciated peasant women and plump matrons; proper young ladies (blossoming saris, college bookbags) and squalid souls keeping something alive there under the tatters; raggedy kids, spiffy kids. No one can escape it. Rheumy-eyed beggars amid lawyers and average bureaucrats. Students with notebooks mixed in with boys their own age who've never been inside a school. Everyone holds onto someone else. Not just the shadows of the Untouchables fall upon the Brahmans, conspicuous by the white cord—unclean breath, sweat, constant touching is their

2

lot also. For seven stops, a social order that considers itself immutable is abolished, its rules are inoperative.

We shall ride this stretch (back and forth) often and become used to it. Already I'm planning techniques for getting on and off. Now—two fingers lashed to the handstrap—I'm roughing out sentences, encapsulated, just as we are encapsulated in our commuter train to Ballygunge.

Whoever travels to India prepares him- or herself. Two people plan a trip to Calcutta, they read. He reads surveys of India's economy, politics, culture, and the contradictory statements about Calcutta; she reads Fontane, always something by Fontane. Don't you want to read something about India before we leave? he asks. I'll get to it, she says, as soon as I've finished this.

But she's not finished with Fontane. Even when she's not reading something by Fontane, she's reading so that she can get back to another Fontane novel. This time, without letup, *Before the Storm.*

During the flight, too, right after the first chicken curry and while an Indian movie is shown in the direction of the cockpit, she reads her Fontane. To keep from reading only about India, he reads what old Chargaff wrote about the coming horrors of genetic engineering, titled *The Invisibly Mended Veil of the Maya.* Casual small talk, suddenly an old man's wicked wit. The movie appears to be an Indian variation of *Schwarzwald Clinic.* He says, while she reads Fontane: Erwin Chargaff calls himself a joyless rider. That applies to me as well.

What I am flying away from: from repetition that claims to be news; from Germany and Germany, the way two deadly foes, armed to the teeth, grow ever more alike; from insights achieved from too close up; from my own perplexity, admitted only sotto voce, flying with me. And from the gobbledygook, the where-I'm-coming-froms, the balanced reporting, the

3

current situations, the razor-elbowed games of self-realization. I am flying thousands of miles away from the superficial subtleties of former leftist now merely chic feuilletonists, and far, far away from myself as part or object of this public exposure.

I know that in Bombay, or in Calcutta at the latest, the adage about wiping your ass with a hedgehog awaits me, just as in the movie up ahead pursuing its hackneyed complications. So, will it be only the climate that is extreme and different? In any case, we've taken precautions against hepatitis, malaria, etc.

Two people read away their fly-away. Beneath them, the Arabian Sea. I'm surfeited on statistics. Ute sticks to Fontane.

On the wall in front of the bishop's manse, along the road to Baruipur, to the right and left of a banyan tree growing from the wall but not bursting it, campaign posters are wooing: the Communist Party CPI(M), with hammer and sickle, and the Congress Party, with a single hand, stylized tantric hands, paint-by-stencil.

Bengali Sunday: on foot in the scramble of the lanes and paths of Baruipur. The poor live next to the comparatively rich, in huts beside ramshackle colonial villas, both grouped around pond-sized puddles, which at present—it is monsoon season—are brimful. In the ooze of the banks, washerwomen; children bathing. Everything, huts and ramshackle villas alike, is wrapped in rank, voracious green and shaded by coconuts. Even the radios blasting at full volume are muted by the homogenizing green. They say there are fish in the ponds. Over toward the railroad embankment, near the Krishna Glassworks, the Untouchables are encamped. Shy curiosity. Misery accustomed to keeping its distance.

Near the bus stop squats a woman in rags, laughing, showing off her newborn, a puny thing, its umbilical cut there in the dust of the road: a boy! (Even we cast only a fleeting glance.)

Just behind the gate, on the path to our summer house, a

4

reptile surprises us. Black, fat, a good yard long, it flees into the undergrowth of banana shrubs. Later, Anvar, the gardener, tells us it's an iguana; occasionally they bite. Anvar and Djanara have an eleven-year-old son, Djerul. A Moslem family. Their hut stands on a slight rise beside the pond.

Still with no subject, just for something to sketch, I draw the interior space of a tree, on whose crisscross of branches the gardener's chickens reside at midday. Gaze from the terrace into the shimmering, otherwise immobile garden in the heat. From the melon bed, shaded by its leaves, creep lewd tendrils, which, this being India, might carry infants instead of melons as their fruit.

Like slack sails the big banana leaves wait for a breeze; they are the first to catch even the faintest puff, usually an empty promise.

Noises of the neighborhood: hammering from some distant workshop, the doleful honks of bicycle rickshas, then the persistent horn of a truck rushing past, or the 208 bus to Calcutta pulls up. Like Anvar the gardener, our neighbor behind the banana bushes also keeps a single duck. Its quacks sound like drawn-and-quartered laughter. In echo, the neighbor's children mimic the laughter of the solitary duck.

In the afternoon—we take the ten-thirty train, a direct commuter from Baruipur—we are hung with garlands. The painter Shuvaprasanna shows us the private art school he runs on Calcutta's north side. In two good-sized rooms, students, cheek by jowl, are set before still lifes. Here, a doll beside a plaster bust of Voltaire; there, a jug with fruit in front of a draped cloth. Among the selected works of several students, large-scale watercolors startle with their Nolde-like colors: groups in fields beneath a towering sky, the goddess Kali with offerings. (Tagore himself, we're told, was thrilled by Nolde's paintings.) I am asked if, at the start of the new year, I

5

will dedicate an artists' colony ("arts acre") near Dum Dum Airport. My half-assent is taken as a full one. Next, group photos . . .

Later, by foot from the Institute to the Park Circus Market: misery, cripples dragging themselves on leather-capped stumps across the cracked pavement. Mangy dogs. The man asleep across our path. Step right over!

Back in Baruipur: a worm on the tabletop, moving forward, first suckerhead, then suckerfoot. Imagine a thousand worms coming at me like that, first suckerhead then suckerfoot . . .

At the river, near the bathing and cremation places, we are passed by four young men in fashionably tight pants, doing double time as they loudly call upon the gods. They carry a bier on which lies an old woman, her eyes covered by leaves about the size of laurel leaves. Each young man wears a wrist-watch. Propelled by the double time to the cremation site, the old woman's head wobbles without displacing the leaves. The flashing watches, the hired shouting.

With us, Shuva the painter. He translates a wall inscription: "Dowries are barbaric!" A new party, calling itself the Renaissance Party, is offering this campaign slogan.

By taxi to Sealdah Station in the chaos of afternoon traffic. The moment we get stuck, the driver's shotgun runs ahead, takes charge of the traffic, directing it like a policeman. Later, in the best of moods, driver and shotgun exchange roles: with success. But all the same we prefer to walk the last lap, wedged in the human throng. Finally through a tunnel where on our left and right sleepers are lying like litter. (A tunnel of panic, made for dreams.)

The neighbor's duck, the tireless laugh-bag. Beneath the humming fan, noonday nap, dreaming northward: of the garden behind the Wewelsflether house, the way its pear trees border the cemetery. And under the largest tree, which year in and

6

year out bears load upon load of gray-green fruit, she sits on the bench at the table, a visitor beside her. Their conversation is pantomimed, true, but my dream dreams an older gentleman (my age), who addresses her, makes her laugh, and in return her laughter invites him—as he talks, explains—can't leave out a single digression!—to smile. And now he laughs, running his fingers through his graying hair combed straight back, reminds me of someone I know. Suddenly, as if by accident, her left hand, the one with rings, is resting on his right forearm, while she talks intensely. It's sure to be another one of her Swedish Hither Pomeranian island stories: from Stralsund, with the sled and lots of schnapps, no wind, across the ice . . .

A good listener, he is. And countering (she's barely delivered her punch line), he has something Brandenburgian, Farther Pomeranian, Mecklenburgian in stock. Engraved tales from Neuruppin.

How well-versed they are in each other. Suddenly the bottle of red wine and the two half-full glasses on the table I dream to be empty, and the man seems older now too, aged to the mid-sixties, worried, dejected, yet certain of her understanding.

The dream dreams a couple for me: Ute and the old Fontane under the pear tree in our garden. And I dream myself behind the closed window, removed, yet close enough to realize: There's something there, something's going on, and for a good many years now. She's carrying on an affair with a much-quoted colleague of yours, in which you do not figure, because his novels (his ballads less so) continue to be worth reading, to be entertaining, more than that, there is exemplary dialogue, take the story "Schach von Wuthenow," in the course of which, using conversations in salons and between people out for a stroll, when the four of them, for instance, walk to Tempelhof Field . . .

My dream dreams it all for me, but also the firm resolve not to fling open the window and shout Enough! or run into

7

the garden as if to the scene of a crime. Instead, I take a glass from the kitchen, grab a chair as I pass, and join them, share their intimacy (on a bench), so that from here on, our three-way love . . .

Then I'm no longer dreaming Ute, Fontane, and me at the table under the pear tree. I lie in sweat. Above, the fan is still. Power outage. The dank heat cripples. Only the laugh-bag is tireless, the neighbor's duck.

. . . and contrary to all reason and heat, today Ute bought wool in a tiny shop, near Ballygunge Station, because the gardener's wife, Djanara, is determined to learn how to knit. Plus three kinds of knitting needles. Out of cashmere skeins of a hundred hues, most of them blended with synthetics, finding the right one. A sweat-producing activity under a motionless ventilator. Despite the close air, the owner of this wool jungle has incense sticks burning beside the cashbox.

Now Djanara is sitting next to Ute on the bench under the terrace roof, learning purl two, knit two. The first Bengali words become familiar. Anvar, little Djerul, and I watch (from manly distance) the knitting miracle. Far up into the night-blackened trees, glowworms sketch tracks of light. My glass of ice water sweats a steadily enlarging puddle.

Addenda under the mosquito net. Next to the meat hall (New Market), an open passageway: for shitting, pissing. Men, before and after they do the shopping. That deft squat. I hold (to no avail) my breath, until I'm through and out.

In the meat hall, next to the butcher stalls for Moslems, a dog trying to wolf down an unborn lamb or kid. The fetus is shiny, smooth, and the way it glistens makes it look fresh and appetizing. But too slippery—the dog has trouble biting into it.

Boned beef at the Moslem butcher stalls costs eleven to thirteen rupees a kilo; lamb (with bones and offal) at the Hindu

8

stalls costs thirty-six to forty rupees a kilo. Not the market, but religion determines the price. (At this writing, one dollar equals twelve rupees, fifty paisa.)

On the way to the Hong Kong Bank, we see a naked woman of indeterminable age propped against a wall. She is covered—as if accidentally—by rags. No one except us seems to notice, and even we slow our pace for only one long terrible second. Beyond begging now. Pariah of pariahs. Pure negligence, that she's still alive. And on walls everywhere—including just to one side of the dying (for how long now?) woman—the hammer and sickle, strangely precise brushwork. After all, West Bengal is governed by Communists and other leftist parties, who have forbidden dying in public.

Is she still alive? Embarrassed questions, posed afterward, over tea, as my German fat sweats away through my pores. Or is she, who was done with us long ago, finally done with herself as well?

Read Lichtenberg's sketchbooks: "If all humans were turned into stone at 3 o'clock one afternoon."

Another moment—no more than a moment—hold it fast: the asphalt-black paddy wagon, incarcerated fingers appearing just under the roof, in the narrow, barred air vents, approximate size three by three inches. As the paddy wagon turns off Park Circus into Mujibar Rahaman Street, not a face, not an eye is visible, only skinny prisoner fingers, addicted to air.

A bicycle ricksha brings us, with detours, from Jodabpur Station right to the door. For a whole evening, enveloped in hospitality. Late, after semisensible chatter about Calcutta's future—the sisal industry, the Bengali cinema, the arduous subway project, and the total inadequacy of the public sewage system—our host accompanies us through the tiny front yard and opens the multibolted gate to the street. There they lie, husband, wife, children, asleep in a row. More sleepers behind, beside them, legs stretched out, propped up, or pulled in, in the curve of the fetal position. The soles of their feet show for identification. Our nocturnal small talk about Calcutta's future is refuted, as it were, by footnotes. . . .

The days pass, without any one assuming a face of its own; they blend into each other, homogenized by the unvarying heat and humidity. It grows increasingly difficult to form thoughts, to cancel the distance. While I read Lichtenberg's sketchbooks and (as befits the Enlightenment) enjoy the humor of failure, a Moslem (and friend of Anvar the gardener) is using the wooden bench on our terrace to stretch himself out for prayers directed to Mecca. The bench, apparently, is in the right position. I watch, while in the dark of the garden, which only the glowworms etch, he disappears in the direction of the tea booth, where time drops away from him, evening after evening.

Actually, we wanted to buy silk. But then in the Great Eastern Hotel, beside the silk shops, we meet this Dutch fellow, who dreams of development projects while at the same time (or incidentally) dealing in silk. After a cup of mocha and cream-cake in the Grand Hotel Oberoi, before whose portals one shift of beggars is replaced by the next, and around whose swimming pool traders and wholesalers—there are hardly any tourists here—drink beer, whiskey, Coke, sloshing it in their glasses, sucking at straws, trying to forget, if only for an hour or so, that Calcutta stands just before the gate—the Dutchman shows us one of the sights of the West Bengal metropolis, at the northern edge of the Maidan, formerly a practice range for Fort William.

Catercorner to the Raj Bhavan, in whose lodges I was the governor's guest eleven years before (like Vasco, a returnee), a small area with a knee-high fence around it attracts an audience. Its surface belongs solely to rats and crows and appears to be sanctified ground. At noon and at the end of the business

10

day, office workers from the firms on Esplanade Row and employees of the Telegraph Office feed the rats and crows potato chips or peanuts, sold by a vendor right next to the enclosure.

We buy peanuts too. Into holes, out of holes no larger than a golf cup, rats scurry. Crows hop, take off, talon the scraps the rats have left behind, just as the rats feast on what the crows have left behind. No squabbles between species. They tolerate one another as peaceably as might have all the beasts in paradise. The crows don't bother with the rats; the rats couldn't care less about the crows. Glad to meet my beasts, I sketch, the moment they hold still. Rats sniffing from golf holes. Restless, beaked black.

I barely begin to count, and I've got better than thirty crows. Rats elude counting. Across the way on Esplanade Row, announced by loudspeaker, a strikers' demonstration begins to form. The employees of an insurance company escalate their wage demands to revolution by repeatedly knocking the head off a straw puppet properly dressed to resemble their boss. Several of the employees look for diversion among the rats and crows, which they feed, the way people elsewhere feed swans and squirrels.

Later, the Dutchman, whose development project promises better market conditions for silk weavers, helps us buy five yards of raw silk, one yard wide.

Theodor Fontane joins in now, not obtrusively though uninvited. He shops with us in the New Market; he comments on the pretty Darjeeling packaging and on the English tea-drinking customs of his day, during his first, second, and third stays in London. He talks me into buying an iron and (what proves more difficult) an ironing board for Ute, who is determined to do the ironing herself despite the humid heat and power outages.

The longer I watch, or we watch—and Fontane is a watching junkie too—the more India (the country whose misery is

11

mystery for the bullshitters, who find everything inscrutable) seems as unmysterious as Denmark (his words). An insipid superstition, this religion. He quotes from his own *Irretrievable*— barbs at pietism.

Cautiously, yet you can't miss it, he begins, if not to retract, then at least to critique his own sympathies for all things English. He is to come along, given his weakness for matters historical, when we visit the Victoria Memorial Museum hulking at the edge of the Maidan.

At last, Ute is reading *Godan*, a novel by the Urdu author Prem Chand. It's about a cow and landless farmers, about crushing interest rates and Brahman arrogance, about workaday, village India, yesterday and today. She reads slowly, as if reading Fontane's *Little Thorn*.

On both forearms, heat rash, especially in the crook of the arm. The trip back in the overcrowded train, standing, walled in, cum ironing board. At Baruipur Station only one old ricksha driver. His naked scrawny back. Even the bicycle bell exhausted. Then, between power outages, in the sultry unstirring garden and later under the mosquito net, reading: *Tallhover*. Hans Joachim Schädlich gave me a copy of the page proofs for the trip.

A book that pursues its thesis with no exit in sight: the virtually immortal agent, spy, secret-service man surviving every system. An expert in matters of state security, who— through the Kaiser's reign, in the Weimar Republic, for as long as the Third Reich lasts, and, with no transition, during the formation of the German Democratic Republic (until June 17, 1953)—unrelentingly performs his official duties. His cause is whatever regime happens to be in power. From this perspective, a hundred years of German history becomes a chronic condition, a file not yet closed, never to be closed.

A sly, simple book, that believes in the fixations of its hero and (apart from some stiff artificial prose at the beginning and the end) takes its language from the world of secret-agentry, which means from events banal and events pregnant with history (Lenin's trip to Russia). Changes of system as smooth transfers from secret file to secret file. Throughout, no individual person emerges. Tallhover develops as a prototype; his private life, except for some hints, is left blank. The reader can either scheme his way into the filing system of that story, or bury it among the dead matter. At the end, the immortal Tallhover condemns himself. A complicated, escalated finale. The (necessarily) precise language of what has gone before now becomes saddled with meaning. The author abandons his hero: Tallhover's decision to die does not ring true. I'll write Schädlich: No, Tallhover cannot die.

After the night's downpours, the taxi takes us through flooded streets from Ballygunge Station to the Institute. There we meet Shuva and a young painter from Assam. I confirm in writing that in January I will dedicate the artists' colony "arts acre" near Dum Dum Airport. Shuva hints at disagreement among the founding members.

Afterward, to the Victoria Memorial Museum, a nightmare hewn in stone, the ultimate evidence of British colonial rule. A domed edifice; before it, the Queen in bronze. We hope to see a documentation of Calcutta's history as a city, of the Indian struggle for independence as well as that of the Bengalis. Likewise the consequences of the rice shortage of 1943, when two million refugees starved in the district of Midnapore, in the Twenty-four Parganas, and on the streets of the city. All we march past, however, are yellowed etchings, the customary massive oils, galleries of imperial ancestors, various curved sabers and daggers, and the moth-eaten uniforms of sepoys. Several curiosities (Lady Curzon's sari), a few documents—a memoir, for instance, in which Warren Hastings informs posterity of his duel with Philip Francis. The issue to be decided: Who would be governor-general? Francis, who shot first, hit Hastings's hat; Hastings wounded Francis in the shoulder and thus held onto his lucrative post. That's how history is made: the absurd reduction of British colonial rule to a "primitive ordeal" (as Schopenhauer calls it in his polemic against duels) between gentlemen on August 17, 1780.

In the Calcutta wing of the museum. The collection is particularly meager; though not totally suppressing Gandhi's importance, it banishes him to its outer fringe. Among a great many photographs, a shot of our Subhas Chandra Bose, whom we've seen as a monument. Here he is in Singapore, in October, 1943, saluting troops of the parading Indian National Army, who are supposed to fight alongside the Japanese Burma Army against British-Indian divisions. Behind Bose stands a Japanese general, saber drawn. Mutton-headed hero worship—for nowhere in this commodious museum is it made clear that there was a conflict between Bose and Gandhi, that Bose openly avowed dictatorship, that he admired Mussolini and Hitler.

Among the all-too-numerous portraits, one attracts us, Philip Burne-Jones's painting (undated) of Rudyard Kipling: in profile at his desk. On his left lies his pipe, at his right hand stands a tennisball-sized globe. In the lower left corner, a full wastebasket testifies to the daily struggle of producing manuscripts. A balding Kipling wears reading glasses and gazes in concentration over their rim into the distance. Atop the bookcase that fills the background—you can't make out any titles—hangs a painting (watercolor?) of a battleship or armed cruiser with two tall smokestacks. All in the style of the New Objectivity.

I want Fontane to tell me—he has come along, as we arranged—whether, as far as his ballads go, he considers Kipling among his successors. To provoke him, I draw a few quick comparisons between Kipling's relationship to the British Empire and Fontane's own love-hate for Prussia. But the old man—this time I see him with snow-white hair, shortly before his seventy-fifth birthday—dodges, calling Ute's attention to

14

several rather incidental documents from the great Lucknow Mutiny of 1857. In 1857, he had been staying, under difficult conditions and not only of a personal nature, in London and Scotland. To be sure, the mutiny and the death of Sir Henry Lawrence, also documented here, had resounded through the forest of English newspapers at the time. In those days Fontane frequented museums with Max Müller, a friend from his youth, from the days when he was still a Herwegh sympathizer and outrageously rebellious, but now Müller was a professor specializing in all things Indian, and consequently an advisor to the Queen and—can you believe it?—recently honored by having the Rhenish-German Cultural Institute in India named after him . . .

For a good while we hear him chatting and grumbling. Several offspring of the heroes of his ballads are portrayed as viceroys. The museum is well-attended: lower-middle-class people, rural families, teachers with pupils. They stand before battle scenes where the English are always the victors.

The lower floor houses an exhibition of the paintings of two artists, Thomas Daniell and William Daniell (uncle and nephew), who arrived in Calcutta by way of China in 1786, remained for six years, and left behind, besides some mediocre harem scenes, several precise, pleasing views of Calcutta, among them a painting by W. Daniell in which the city, seen from the river, resembles Venice. Current flooding, following recent monsoon downpours, confirms the resemblance.

Later, after grueling detours, we visit a sociologist, whose team is researching the living conditions of ricksha pullers (suspension of licenses) and slum dwellers, particularly those living along canals and railroad embankments. We eat fish, rice, mashed lentils, and oversweet dairy dishes. Our museum visit doesn't interest the sociologists. That history is counterfeit. People have other problems.

On the platform at Ballygunge Station—we have almost an

hour to wait—one of the many beggars approaches us. Legs amputated above the knee, he slides on worn leather pads, points his empty tin can at us. I want to put a two-rupee bill in the can, but grab the wrong one—the same red color, but a little larger—twenty rupees. The crippled man's alarm. He quickly sees to it that the bill vanishes from his can, stares at us for a long time, not moving, turns abruptly, skids off on his padded knees, but a little later rows himself again our way, very close, and repeatedly presents us with a folded paper, a typed and stamped certification by a police commissioner that this cripple is an honest man: Has known the man for twenty years. For ten years now, following an accident, handicapped, with a family, etc.

Standing in the commuter train's compact mass, the overburdened handstraps the only hold, everyone is silent. For them we're as alien as we are close. On arrival in Baruipur—even though the fans have been running—Ute collapses. It is too much, too much every day, and no one, not Fontane himself, can help.

Very early, just as yesterday, but today accompanied by thunder and cloudbursts, a radio bellows at full volume somewhere nearby, as if to demonstrate its recent purchase. Not much farther off, another radio with another program. Both stations, outshouting each other, have the same tone of voice: the sweet refrains of Indian film and pop music—but now above light steady rain.

The flies here have a squat, powerful build and resolute colors. The body green-black; the head, including ocular equipment, rich red. Their unblemished colors accompany our breakfast. Recently a newspaper has been arriving daily: *The Telegraph.*

From Lichtenberg to Schopenhauer: *Parerga and Paralipomena.* The text segues seamlessly into all the horrors of the present. (As a seventeen-year-old in Toulon—on an educational

16

trip—he saw galley slaves in chains, and his view of humanity was primed; all it needed now was the painting.)

After which, we use the morning to go by bicycle-ricksha to the post office in Gobindapur. No letters, but soundlessly circling vultures above the town, a scattered rural settlement set in rank green. Rice fields among ponds. Everywhere now the altars for Durga Puja, the coming festival. And in contrast to the vultures, bawling loudspeakers.

Exhausted, back from Calcutta. (By Catholic reckoning, every train ride should be counted as remission of sins.) Ute's disgust at everything she has to touch, to smell. She takes a long shower. I sit in my sweat, drink ice water that was boiled first, smoke a cigarillo. Frogs, crickets, the neighbor's duck. Thank God: no radios.

Craniums of green coconuts that are struck open with a machete, and the milk, as well as the soft fleshy fruit, is considered healthy, is said to heal rashes and blisters. They lie empty wherever green coconuts are sold for fast consumption, and as trash where the other trash swells the municipal garbage. They are layered in heaps so suggestively that I see decapitated heads among them, here Hindus, there Moslems, as they were lying piled high—and not only in the year of independence, beginning, sharp as a machete, with India's partition—on the streets of Calcutta, in Kalighat, and at Park Circus, near Lalbazar and even on College Street, and will be piled again soon enough.

Using straws that we assume are unused, we drink the green nuts empty, to avoid tap water. (The climate demands six quarts of liquid a day.) A woodchip makes a spoon for the meat. Tastes insipid, but refreshes.

At street corners, in front of movie houses, temples, by gas stations, by brightly painted sugarcane presses, and in the throngs outside Ballygunge Station. Next to the coconuts, it is often Kali herself with her crescent-moon machete, squatting

17

just as everyone squats here: on her heels, in arm's reach of her wares. With a few strokes she opens the fruit as it hops between blows. Practice makes perfect. (She wields the machete in twelve-armed style only in legends and gaudy illustrations.) Suddenly she shows her tongue: a head, male. Another head, bald, hidden under fruit sucked empty, spooned empty. (We, looking for compensation, conjecture heads of corrupt politicians or a Brahman who got in her way.)

A rapidly changing clientele, not just from nearby. A child who collects everything gathers up used straws. The growing golgotha. Later crows atop it, who constantly pull new crows down from the sky. At closeout sale prices, black ones.

Dhapa, a spacious landscape invented from layers of garbage. Canyons hewn in the garbage that has been turned over and over; nothing dare be lost. The crows, vultures, goats, and the dump trucks arriving from the city day and night—for of garbage there is no end—are part of the landscape. Everything— who collects what, who delivers what, who is allied with which dump truck, who passes what on and to whom, who jobs it and knows when the loaded trucks will arrive from the hotels and hospitals—everything, not just the strikes of the garbage collectors, is organized.

Among the Garbage Mountains, a barracks is used for a school; there, the garbage children, earnest, concentrating, learn words that have meaning only in another world (or landscape), a world far away, beyond the Seven Hills of Garbage. . . .

In one of the villas from colonial days, though entrusted now to decay, live Mrs. and Mr. Karlekar. They come from Brahman families, but that was long ago, forgotten, like childhood diseases. All her life, she trained teachers; he was in ship construction. Now they are well past seventy; ten years ago they set up a school and kindergarten in the neighboring slum of Monoharpukur and then forged on to Dhapa, into the Gar-

18

bage Mountains. Their organization is called the Calcutta Social Project. Against the opposition of the Communist Party, which has political control over this area as well, they were finally assigned a place for their project and given a license for their school. Many of the garbage children come from peasant families who raise vegetables, most conspicuously cauliflower, on the older garbage, which after three monsoon seasons turns to humus.

We join the old couple for a ride in a rickety jeep to the neighboring slum, then to Dhapa. Under the porch roof of the school barracks, about thirty small children squat on bast-fiber mats, watched over by older children. In the shade of the walls, an altar: three smooth egg-shaped stones.

Learning in progress in every classroom, as if knowledge could move mountains, as if all mountains were mere mountains of garbage. Several of the young teachers (at a monthly salary of three hundred fifty rupees) were once pupils in the slum school at Monoharpukur. Later the children dance for us, dances in which farm work—sowing, hoeing, reaping, threshing—determine the movements. After that, a dance accompanied by what sounds like English recitative, in the course of which a patient is examined by a doctor, operated on, and healed. The children's solemnity offsets the humor of the presentation.

By now the flies, the stench, the vultures circling above the school in the middle of the Garbage Mountains, have become familiar, part of the scene.

From the tales of the gods. Her sickle raised in a right hand attached to one of her ten arms, Kali, in frenzy, shows her tongue when (perhaps by a shout from the wings) she is made aware that she is preparing to go for the throat of her divine spouse Siva, who, like Kali, is a god of destruction. Showing her tongue, a sign of shame. Since then, Kali has been available in illustrated form: as a painted clay figure, on shiny posters,

19

ten-armed, ten-footed, often with multiple heads, ditto the tongue. The banner unfurls, showing her colors. While all around her, so the legend, her attendants, ten thousand raging females, are busy winding up the off-with-their-heads job, she hesitates, spares the sleeping and, as always, unsuspecting god, allows him to keep the blissful smile of his dreams, and shows her credentials.

Reminiscent of Einstein in the well-known photograph. Reporters are said to have provoked him. His tongue—like Kali's—is excessively long. Quite apart from the panting pushiness of a gang that delights in living off private garbage, it could be that shame likewise prompted Einstein to show his tongue.

He and the black goddess together on a giant poster. Or I imagine a conversation in which they exchange experiences on the topic of nowadays vs. Last Days. Site for their chat: Dhapa, Calcutta's garbage dump. Among the garbage children. Crows and vultures above. Both balance the world's accounts, its final increment. A dump truck arrives, unloads. The children search, find, and show them. Einstein and Kali compare their tongues. Photo opportunity. The garbage children laugh.

Built of brick, roofed with tile, great slums called bustees, for decades now, some even dating back to the days of British rule, are an integral part of Calcutta. Quite different, the small and medium-sized slums pushed out of the central city along railroad tracks and major arteries. Those arise as if overnight, made of tents, crates, fragile huts, and they vanish suddenly, grow up elsewhere, along sewage channels or next to new developments. Near Dhapa for instance, on the main road that feeds into Dum Dum Airport: shoved up against the roadbank, supported by a waist-high wall, a slum run riot, ducking beneath the two smokestacks (the fumes angry black) of an adjacent factory.

Struggling apart, slightly askew, supported by cables, sheltered by pointed caps, they are smokestacks from the nineteenth

20

century, when Engels was describing the condition of the working class in England. Here they are in our time, a time accustomed to quick good-byes, moving so swiftly away from itself that it becomes unrecognizable. Ignore the misery—custom invites you to ignore it—and the slum is part and parcel of the factory and of its daily expectoration: roofs of layered tar paper, scraps of plastic, plywood, leftover tiles, stuffed with rags, each its own distinct tangle. Sacks, straw mats weighed down with stones and sticks, tin rusting on tin, tires on top, flabby hoses, a car hood rolled flat. And jammed together: baskets, sieves, crates. Tied up in wire, sisal ropes. Layer on layer of chance, items found by chance—wretchedness, or wealth of a different sort.

If you lent (for a fee) one of these slum hovels, created from bare necessity, to the city of Frankfurt am Main, and had it set down next to the Deutsche Bank highrise, where the hewn granite sculpture by the artist Bill says yes, always yes to the towering bank, because as an endless loop it loves only itself, is incontrovertibly beautiful and immaculately endorses the circulation of money stamped valid for eternity—if, I say, you replaced that granite celebrating its flawless self, and set down instead one single slum hovel, as authentic as want has made it, right next to the glassy arrogance of the Deutsche Bank, beauty would at once be on the side of the hovel, and truth too, even the future. The mirrored art of all those palaces consecrated to money would fall to its knees, because the slum hovel (each hovel in its own way) belongs to tomorrow.

On, past the many open fires between and in front of the sheds along the road that bypasses Dhapa on the east. Yellow-gray smoke lies over the slum, unraveling, a blanket in shreds.

Ahead of us lies a drive of a hundred and ten miles, and the return. Our goal is Vishnupur in West Bengal, which appears as Bishnupur on our road map. Shuva and his wife Sipra have booked a rental car for six in the morning.

21

For the first time there's a driver at the wheel who is blind to the potholes and the go-slow ties, these usually in groups of three, tumors athwart the pavement, caesuras for speeders, a device used in every town. Forty miles from our goal, the motor goes on strike. Six, seven times, we have to stop in a village or on the open road until the driver, by sucking, spitting, blowing into the gas lines, manages to cajole it into a good mood for the next few miles. Not until we reach Vishnupur does a mechanic replace the spark plugs and whatever. But the car, resuming its steady decline, will lose trimmings from the left front wheel on the trip back.

A nervous Shuva can quarrel (to no avail) with the driver all he likes, we enjoy our stops on the country road and in the villages. The traffic of oxcarts and pedestrians. Beneath loads on their heads, old women clutch sticks and branches to their sides, the daily firewood. Children out searching for wood as well, peasant girls with a lateral ring on their noses. We are told that every day each family sends out one or two members to roam over many miles. Which is why there are so many children, why the forests are dying, why nothing grows again, except children.

The trees along the road show no signs of damage. Under a wide-spreading tree, a man squats between knees jutting upward, drawing geometric forms in the sand, triangles—pointed at the top, at the bottom—and, bouncing stones in his free hand, mutely lures passersby to his game. No one wants to play with him. He erases the drawing, abandons his squatting position, and walks off with his playthings. Between one breakdown and the next, we drink green coconuts dry.

At last, in Vishnupur. A typical small town, but alongside this one is a complex of temples built between the tenth and seventeenth centuries. At one time, as a political and religious center, it was set within fortified walls, of which only a few towers and the main gate still stand. Defended by jungle and water, it never fell under Moslem rule, as did extensive areas

22

of Bengal and Orissa. (Despite the enthusiasm Shuva brings to his knowledge of the temple complex, his explanations are nothing but the warmed-over hash of art history.) The tourist lodge—a government operation, where we wash up and eat fish, rice, and the mashed lentils they call dhal, all served by languid waiters—awakens memories of trips in countries of the East Bloc. Beneath the whirring fan in the room where we wash up, the only running water is scalding hot.

The temples lie in a landscape that evokes melancholy. The remains of earthworks, dilapidated huts, goats among overgrown rubble—with primitive facilities to further tourism. The entrance portal to the temple area is set up with metal turnstiles that allow only one person at a time to enter, as if massive throngs were expected in the near future.

Of the four temples, the most impressive are the two in terra-cotta, with their integrated form, the variety of the figured and ornamented tiles. Jor Bangla is a double temple, its mushroom roofs similar to those of Bengali farmhouses in the region (some of them two-storied, bamboo-framed affairs). The red glazed clay, fired to different degrees of hardness, varies in hue and saturation. Even those tiles gnawed and battered by weather are still alive, each in its own way. The cheerful cult of Krishna romps from brick to brick. And him, always with flutes, animals, and women. The animals are represented in a simple but in no way primitive style. Far from all mystification and ambiguity, the legends pictured here tell of a sensual religion. Everything has a human scale and, despite its formalized framework, is abidingly playful. Later we notice that there are no potter's workshops to be seen along the borders of the temple complex. No heritage of handicrafts has remained from this culture.

In front of the Rash Mancha temple, a basalt pyramid jacketed by galleries, a square opens up, where beneath tall trees cockfights are held. Narrow the field of vision. The pyramid pulls away; the cocks, immense now, are placed opposite one

23

another, their combs vertical. Leave out (in my drawing) the circle of wagering spectators. To one side lie the heads and feet of vanquished cocks. Before the fight, the precious knife of the spur is kept wrapped. Cocks waiting in cages.

Down the road, where the town begins with the customary piles of garbage, two monkeys do gymnastics in tall trees, endless mazes of branches. Crowds of men, only men, in white cotton, return from some sports event; earnest, taciturn, as if the wrong team has won. And here, too, in a public square, Subhas Chandra Bose: just a bust, not on horseback. (In 1938, shortly after his return from Europe, Bose chaired a Congress Party conference in Vishnupur.)

It has taken eight hours to get here. A return trip by night frightens us. (The potholes, the go-slow ties, the surly indifference of the man at the wheel.)

Then moonlight lies on all ponds. My thoughts, can't turn them off, are with Schädlich's *Tallhover*. Endless variations on the novel's ending: Tallhover, immortal, now lives in the West, introduces new methods of identification, intensifies searches via the grid system. . . .

. . . around midnight, at last in the circle of Five Point Crossing, where bespectacled "Netaji" rides in bronze toward Delhi, through the north side of Calcutta. The bustling hell. There they lie: pavement dwellers pushed out of the central city, vomited up from the countryside (Bengal, Bihar, Orissa), whom no slum will have or hold, who have nothing but the pavement, on both sides of the main road to Sealdah Station and beyond. They lie banked along the facades, in shadows or dimly lit by a few arc lamps (those still working), for a film that no one will make. Sleepers arranged by family, solitary sleepers, stray dogs here and there. Cows, sacred and restless, guarding this sleep.

Everyone sleeps a different sleep. Limbs stretched or folded. Bodies wrapped like mummies or under coverings that are too

24

short. Rows of child-bundles. Obstructed by sacks of garbage, by bundles of old paper, they multiply in their sleep. Bony and pale, a calf towers into view.

All this seen from the middle of the road—the pictures jolt out of focus with each bounce. Sudden light rips open facades, slashes the darkness. Tea shops, still open, are wrenched askew, as are the markets, open for Durga Puja. Everything plummets, the garish arc lamps plummet too, as if an Expressionist had invented this rush of streets for a woodcut of epileptic collapse. Only the sleepers remain real, though from centuries past. Veiled or openmouthed, they lie there while time and its harbinger, progress, send everything sliding in an avalanche in their direction.

Among the thousands of sleepers, however, we see one awake, reading by faint light. Pious mantras, or a Bengali version of Donald Duck. Nonstop poetry by Tagore, or some pamphlet for the future: Netaji's return on a white horse, as whispered by legends?

The reader in the midst of sleep (and the dreams of the thousand sleepers) is overwhelmed by traffic noise. Trucks, one after the other, "Mother Dairy" milk tankers, loaders full of gravel pounding the road. And in between, bundles of bamboo rods on carts pushed by shouting men, men setting their compact, muscular bodies against the oversized freight. Only by night do they deliver this cumbersome material for scaffolds and grandstands.

And the sleepers, death sleepers, who soon will live again, lie pressed beneath the exhaust fumes of a neverending day.

Everything molds: shoes, pipes, those last cigarettes; back to back, the books . . .

In sketchbook L, Lichtenberg writes: "People speak of enlightenment, and want more light. My God, of what use is light to men who have no eyes or, if they have eyes, who willfully close them?" In the same sketchbook, the same Lich-

25

tenberg over and over again expresses contempt for the Jews as a people—for instance, by applauding the expulsion of several Jewish families from Göttingen, or when he acknowledges Moses Mendelssohn, whom he held in personal esteem, only within the context of Mendelssohn's intellectual milieu (Berlin). But then even he calls the Jews "worthless fruit that does not thrive in another climate."

The question of the origins of anti-Semitism and its consequences, all the way to the Wannsee Conference and Auschwitz, cannot be answered by pointing to a lack of enlightenment, not when one of the keenest minds of the Enlightenment, right in the midst of perceptions still valid today, emerges as a stubborn anti-Semite. Why has this side of my Lichtenberg, who loves to quote Lessing, remained hidden from me till now? And in his wake, is Fontane's ironic, patronizing amiability when dealing with Jews (and his review of Gustav Freytag's anti-Semitic novel *Debit and Credit*) of comparable obtuseness?

Early this morning (at breakfast with the flies), the author of a lengthy *Telegraph* article entitled "India in the Year 2001" hopes that computerization will put an end to administrative corruption and that a just land reform will finally be initiated. Enlightenment as superstition.

She no longer reads Fontane. He wipes mold from book bindings. She irons laundry to take to Puri. He hopes that the city of temples may give her a little pleasure, do her good, help. A week at the ocean. We picture wide beaches. Away from Calcutta. Get some air. The Puri Express is leaving this evening from Howrah Station.

I've finished *Parerga and Paralipomena*, to the extent anyone can ever finish this summation, this balancing the accounts of a lifetime of experience. Hitting the mark every time, he delights in proving that nothing is certain, that you can depend on nothing, that nothing lasts, and then nullifies his evidence by raising the principle of material security to the status of a

26

maxim, painfully reckoning everything down to the penny. As he makes provisions for countering life's blows, his own thrifty management of inherited wealth glints through. Boldly and mercilessly he pounds home his polemics, grabbing mediocrity and its clichés by the collar—but then gives some anxious, vague advice about "saving for a rainy day." After the grand opening (where he unmasks all the bugbears and like a circus director leads every human bestiality before the audience), the bottom line remains a petit-bourgeois morality. My assessment, in any case, from Calcutta.

Djanara, the gardener's wife, whines that Ute, whom she calls Didi or older sister, will be gone too long. She wants to knit a shawl for Djerul, just as she's learned in her knitting lessons held each evening. Now that Ute's bladder infection seems to be cured, let's hope her earaches subside too. The sum of these everchanging ailments, their discomforts often simultaneous, is worrisome. (She no longer allows her temperature to be taken; he has few, far too few suggestions to relieve her unspoken suffering.) Maybe the week in Puri will help. Those beaches keep widening in our imaginations.

Reading Schopenhauer after Lichtenberg invites comparisons. Both are pessimists, yet Lichtenberg takes no pleasure in skeptical insights; he remains open, curious, capable of passion. Schopenhauer, on the other hand, sits atop his collected findings, directing the reader's attention to them, referring to his "World As Will and Idea" and early treatise on "Freedom of the Will," wanting to prove himself right and—annoyingly enough—proving it, however scornfully his truths laugh.

After a restless night in the sleeping car, through the federal state of Orissa. It's raining. In the fields, men stand under bast hoods that reach to their knees. Here, too, the pan-Indian morning ceremonial: washing in public, squatting to shit at the edge of fields, along railroad embankments, in ditches. Around the pumps at the train stations, too. In contrast, the fastidious,

27

almost cultlike cleaning of the teeth. The landscape repeats itself region after region.

Puri is a town trimmed to the needs of the pilgrims and beggars of the temple of Jagannath. Booths, cookshops, and hordes of monkeys along the temple walls. Gods and demons painted lurid colors, all making faces, frame the gate: no admittance for unbelievers. Above the Jagannath tower—a curlicued, encrusted penis—monsoon clouds scud menacingly. Comparisons to Catholic places of pilgrimage are all too easy: fed by universal fear and despair, faith in a motley humbug.

From the hotel terrace we look out to the sea, the surf. Colonial furniture. Soundless waiters, uniformed, turbaned. We are surrounded by the restored charm of what once were third-class British accommodations. Only a few guests at dinner; a blend of bad Indian and normal English cooking. An arrogant, unfriendly Brahman plus fat wife, a younger Italian couple, two Americans poking at their food. (To animate the table-to-table conversation, we should have brought along Fontane.)

In the bar, an abandoned lending library offers a bookcase full of thumbed potboilers in English. Among them are books by Subhas Chandra Bose. Paging, I read of his rejoicing in German military victories; this was written in 1940, shortly before he fled to Europe.

On the television, an Indian soap opera. The moment we seat ourselves in the colonial chairs, the trap snaps shut—we become English, we talk like the English, too: indifferent, supercilious. The cats here are as ugly as the dogs.

In front of the hotel, old men wearing pointed fishing caps wait for guests who want to swim in the surf; they are persistent in their offers of help. Seen from close up, the beach, wide though it may be, is full of shit wherever you step—sometimes pale, crumbly, dry, sometimes black-brown, runny. Extending out of sight to the east, a fishing village, where during the fishing season (from September until early January) over ten

28

thousand people crowd in on top of one another. After which, the harvest draws a portion of the men and women into the country.

Boats of roughly hewn planks are kept bound together through their bungholes. We watch the fisherman skillfully bring their boats to shore at noon. They steer not with rudders but with broad spoon-paddles. Off to one side, two young fellows in the surf pull a net between poles. All along the beach, broods of children. Spray over everything.

Across from the hotel, an open sewer divides the beach, filling up at high tide and flowing in a strong current to the sea when the tide goes out. I watch men fishing in the sewer. They alternate two nets as they work. While one man gleans the catch from one net, five hold the other against the current. Out of the slime and garbage, out of the shit of Puri's pilgrims and beggars, they gather fish the size of one's little finger, which, if they fish long enough, will suffice for one meal. They hardly speak, rarely call from net to net. In front of them, beyond the gibbous beach, the sea pounds. But they dare not spread their nets in the sea itself, like those young fellows outside the village; these are Untouchables, they belong to the sewer, they are the sewer. A life sentence.

From beneath the palm trees whose loose ranks shade the Eastern Railway Hotel, you can't see the sewer fishers. But I know they're there. No one, no faith healer using his statistics, no lover of Indian profundities, no gentle Indologist for whom everything, the sewer included, is reconciled in some eternal order, can babble them away for me. It is teatime. With the ugly cats lurking on all sides, and with no transition, as if one hell borders the next (Schopenhauer), I read Canetti's *Auto-da-Fé*, secure in my colonial chair.

The next day, we rent a car and drive with the Italian couple to Konarak, to the Sun Temple, also called the Black Temple. At breakfast, before we leave, *The Statesman* reports that Shuva, who in fact wanted to meet us here in Puri with his art students

29

(looking for subjects), has been arrested. One of his students committed suicide and in the suicide note accused him of embezzling money the Foundation was to use for its "arts acre." During the investigation, Shuva will have to remain in custody. (The newspaper likewise reports that Calcutta is threatened by floods. A tropical storm over the Bay of Bengal is said to be to blame.) I don't want to visit the Sun Temple; I would rather be in Calcutta now.

Parallel to the sea, we drive through a flat region forested with regularly planted, long-needled young firs. Pia and Emilio come from Bergamo; she is an art teacher, he an agronomist. The temples lie in a circle of shading trees. Behind the first temple, whose upper part is a ruin, a second temple represents a chariot, with twenty-four wheels hitched to horses in front. The wheels and the figured ornamentation—elegant masonry and sculpture from the thirteenth century—are badly weathered and, at the rear, so ravaged that a portion of the temple resembles a quarry. In niches large enough for a small child to stand in, couples engage in chiseled love, as if meant to illustrate the *Kama Sutra*. Emilio loads a new roll of film. Pia looks for shade. Ute has a fever, she shivers in the sun. I watch the masons, who have been hired to combat the decay of the temple.

At a stop on the drive home, we walk along the beach as far as the outlying huts of a fishing village. The last boats are returning. Each beaching is a struggle. Several boats capsize and are righted again out in the surf. Because sails, nets, and catch are all roped together, nothing gets lost. Tumults along the beach, since the catches are immediately claimed by the boat owners and bought up by fish dealers. Arguments between fishermen and dealers. The alien language, the obvious gestures. A frightening number of kids, who, the minute they spot us, start begging. (Emilio buys a good-sized fish, which the hotel chef will prepare for us later.) Here, too, as in the fishing village near the Eastern Railway Hotel, the beach is full of shit. More boats are coming in, but Pia and Ute have had enough. . . .

On the terrace, drinking tea. The waiters shoo the cats, whom tea biscuits lure back again and again. Sitting in a colonial chair, reading *Auto-da-Fé*—a book whose steep descent signals the catastrophe from the start, anticipating the inevitable outcome and as a result slackens the tension: the library goes up in flames because the book has been laid on the pyre.

Pia and Emilio depart. With them goes one of our buttresses: Europe. The flood in Calcutta fills three pages of the *Statesman*. Photos show hip-deep flood marks in the streets. A special report on the Kamartuli quarter of the city, where the ceramic workers have their workshops: the persistent rains have ruined many clay figurines of the gods—with Durga Puja upon us— dissolving them. Only because our sleeping-car reservations can't be changed (so we are told), are we still here.

Other items in the paper: the Asian Games have been going for days now. For India, some bronze, a little silver, no gold. And again, the quotidian terror: the Sikhs, the Gurkhas, decapitations in Bihar. And every day we read about young women whose saris catch fire while they are cooking. As a rule it's the mothers-in-law who do them in, doing their sons a favor because of an insufficient dowry.

Along the asphalt road to Puri that leads to the temple, where a billboard of pilgrims on motorcycles promises modern tours, we see a long-haired, bearded sadhu, face and arms painted, who has covered much ground by lying down, standing up, lying down—advancing each time by one body length. The pilgrim's journey reminds me of that worm I watched in Baruipur, as it moved by worm lengths toward me.

By now the district of Midnapore and the Twenty-four Parganas have been flooded as well. Pakistan has defeated India in hockey three to one. We leave the sea and the surf behind us. Not a glance back. All those cows before the train station: horned patience.

Shuva, released from pretrial custody two days before, meets us as our train pulls in at night. He's doing fine, so many friends, students, it will all sort itself out. The battle for a taxi to Baruipur. The city is setting its house in order after the flooding. Work gangs against sludge. Gravel to fill the bigger potholes. People standing in long lines for kerosene. In the lower parts of the city, the water still knee-high. Wading, newspaper boys hawk the *Telegraph*. In the Midnapore district, dams have broken.

And the ponds in Baruipur are spilling over. Djerul shows us the high-water mark. Some rain damage in the house. New mold on all the book spines. Chickens again, on long legs around the table. The way their heads jerk when they stand still. Different positions of the beak, without transition, as if from some patched and repatched film. Djanara's broom, leaning against the wall, pushes itself into the picture.

Later I work on the poem. Exhausted, Ute sleeps. From afternoon into the night, heavy rain. The word "downpour" fits.

Today, at the Institute, a young man accosts me, modest, soft, but determined. A lyric poet and journalist, he was banished from Bangladesh ten years ago because of a poem. Since then, in Calcutta, on a visa fitfully extended. He offers to show us the city, down to its remotest, blackest corners. His name is Daud Haider. We make an appointment.

Then a quick glance at the German dailies, which are a week old, even older. The *Süddeutsche*, the *Frankfurter Allgemeine*. The vast hole in the social security system; arguments about "Neue Heimat," the federally supported now bankrupt public housing that is to be unloaded (residents included)—a major political

32

scandal (Socialist); the mountains of grain, beef, butter; carping from Bavaria, Social-Democratic neither/nor, Herr Rau's trenchant Bible quotes, the chancellor's collected verbal flatulence . . . Quickly, all too hastily, I turn back to Calcutta.

Burdens carried as though free of gravity. Children culling half-consumed lumps of coal from garbage dumps. They use sticks to knock off the ashy grit. Later we watch as they wash the collected pieces in shallow basins at the roadside. A new product. Nothing is wasted.

First to the temple of Kali, into the holy of holies. Next, Daud Haider leads us to Calcutta's oldest bathing and cremation facility, right beside the pier for the ferry to Howrah on the other side of the Hooghly River: the Nimtallah Ghat. Just as many Bengalis are not bashful about pushing up close to us, wanting to see, to touch everything, showing no fear of body contact except within their caste system, so now, too, they let us watch as they bathe, are massaged, and burn their corpses. But without Daud along, we would not have risked entering the temple, moving in among the bathers, drawing close to the pyres.

All three sites have old garbage and fresh garbage in common. Kali, a bogeywoman in black granite, adorned by the priests with gold glitter and flowers, is showered by more and more glitter and flowers as the pilgrims, who have been standing in long lines outside, are finally led into the orbit of the "Terrible Mother." The temple attendants guide and push the neverending throng, collecting money at the various entrances. With all the others, we too walk barefoot over mangled flowers. Shove, are shoved, slip on slick soles. From our feet, mounting nausea, horror. We've had enough; but Daud (laughing) wants us to watch. The odor of stale flowers clings to us with persistence. In front of the temple: beggars, prostitutes, booths full of devotional kitsch, the bustle of shopping.

At the bathing facility, a fat man's back is being walloped by the knees of a masseur while the fat man bites on a stick that many before him have bitten. On the steps down to the river, people sit, waiting, the brackish brew still ahead of them. The slow movements of the bathers, slowed as if by dream. In the loamy yellow water of the Ganges drift fecal matter, floral wreaths, single blossoms, charred wood. Set distant now by a river breadth, the industrial plants of Howrah. Sky daubed with smoke banners and monsoon clouds. In the anteroom of the bathing area: towel rental, betel vendors, also opium pipes on display next to head scarves, plastic bowls.

The crematorium has a special department for electrical incineration. Two corpses wrapped in cloths—a young man, an old woman—surrounded by family. In an adjoining building, which serves as an inn, groups are crouching, some sleeping, waiting their turn. As everywhere on Calcutta's north side, the architectural style of the buildings is Victorian, with an admixture of Indian detail. Someday Nimtallah Ghat will be protected by landmark status, even if it takes the assistance of the World Bank.

In one of the crematory courtyards, all of them open to the river, a male corpse burns within a pile of wood. Two other pyres give off labored, smudgy smoke, because the wood is still wet from the recent floods. Reinforcements of brushwood, kerosene. The smoke, indolent, loiters. Along with his helpers, the Brahman, a grimy bald man, keeps trying to fan the fire. On a pyre farther down, an old woman, not yet covered by the crisscross of wood, lies amid the farewells—howls that begin and end abruptly—of her daughters and grandchildren. Sticking out from under the shroud, head, shoulders, the feet. Because they are rubbed with ghee, clarified butter, the exposed limbs and the fleshless skull-like head glisten. More garlands thrown on. The flat smoke of the neighboring fire drifts slowly, very slowly, down to the river.

Not even the ceremonial howling dampens the workaday, almost cheerful mood. Along the front of the row of bathing and cremation buildings are booths, tea kitchens, and huts

34

where prostitutes wait. Among the shifting throngs, fidgety goats and cows. Behind them, the tracks of the Circular Rail, and freight trains moving. On the other side of the railroad— the crossing safeguarded by a double gate—narrow slum, leaning against factory walls, runs parallel to the tracks. Daud Haider explains that more and more slums are forming along railroad tracks since there is no other place for them.

Behind the track crossing, where Nimtallah Ghat Street begins, and towering above the huts of the slum, piles of stacked wood for sale as fuel for cremations. As I sketch, I find order in the tangle of timber. Bald branches, pale flayed trunks. The wood is weighed out on metal scales. Only the rich can afford sufficient wood. The free-market economy, death as an overhead expense, like everywhere else.

Off to Alipore, where the rich reside and the consuls with their spouses have cloistered themselves for ease of social visits. The suburb dates back to Warren Hastings, who built his villa here and had the marble for his staircase brought from Benares. We visit the National Library, the former residence of the British viceroy. Over a million books, all exposed to Calcutta's special climate, the director jokes, and points to air-conditioned quarters in the new annex.

The Victorian reading room: stalwart tables, reading lamps of antiquarian charm, comfortable chairs, as if colonial power intended to stay on forever and ever. And everywhere (as everywhere in the world) students: suggestive of application, of interest, even. During their student days, Daud, his friend Sourav, and Sourav's wife, Tripaty, who have joined us, found all their sourcebooks on Indian and Western literature here. (All in English. Neither Daud nor Sourav, who is also a writer, can read poems written in Urdu or Tamil.)

In the spacious stacks, through whose channels we are rapidly towed, six underpaid library employees lead the battle (defeat already conceded) against the mold-producing climate, frequently interrupted by the consumption of tea or preparations for their next strike.

On to the modern annex—which, lacking Victorian trimmings, needs no commentary on its international ugliness—where rare, often unique, books, scrolls, and manuscripts have found rescue in climate control. We look at Tamil script etched on narrow strips of palm leaf.

In an institution tended so carefully for reasons of state, the filth, strewn about or in piles, is particularly eye-catching. Just endure it: the primal stench of the men's toilet right next to the cafeteria. But what compels the studious young ladies of Bengal, always fresh as blossoms in their saris, to throw their sanitary napkins on the floor of the women's toilet? There are piles of them, Ute reports, and her eyes, all Pomeranian censure, pursue the graceful daughters of the ambitious middle class.

Later, Daud leads us to the Behala Manton slum on the city's west side. Within its small quarters, perhaps sixty by two hundred yards, live more than six thousand people, four thousand of whom are children. In stalls roomier than the huts, booths, and sheds, stand about a hundred black milk cows in resident swarms of flies. The slum and the cows belong to a man who lives outside Calcutta and exacts between fifty and a hundred rupees per month per hut. Barely eighteen inches wide, the passageways between the huts are open sewers that empty, to the right, into a long canal filled with the torpid cloacal tide. I see only one water pump; I'm told there is a second, by the cows.

Only one child, who is proudly displayed to us, goes to school. A quarter of the adults have found employment: as sweepers or ricksha pullers. An invitation, energetic but friendly, to look inside the hovels. Six, seven people to a shack. Because of the daily danger of floods during the monsoon season, the beds—or, rather, the common bed—is raised on bricks. It takes up most of the room. Under the bed, beneath

36

a patchwork blanket, and in a lean-to nook lie, hang, are piled the paltry possessions: shiny aluminum pots, water jugs, storage jugs. Everything emphatically clean, the stamped clay floor swept, the pillows on the family bed, five or seven of them, neatly lined up. And always attended by divinities, in brightly colored pictures. I would maintain that these wretched asylums, Calcutta's millions of slum huts, are cleaner than the rest of the city's chaotic checkerboard: a desperate cleanliness, wrested from misery.

When, shortly before Durga Puja, virtually every quarter of the city stood under water, the Behala Manton slum was also evacuated. Only a few of the huts collapsed, they tell me. But the passageways, the open sewers between the rows, and the main lateral lanes are still nothing but a morass. Yet crowds, hordes of children, water bearers, all sorts of burdens carried on heads, burdens that, no matter how bulky and projecting, manage to make it past one another. Above all this, the acrid smoke of open fires fed with cakes of dried cow dung.

As everywhere else in the city, the women and children here too follow in the wake of the cows, collect the dung, dump it into tubs, mix it with chopped rice straw and coal dust, make a paste, and from the paste make cakes that are pressed to dry on the walls. Each cake imprinted by fingers, the fingers of women and children. In every quarter of the city, even near Park Street, on the walls of the old English cemetery, on culverts tall as men, next to the subway construction sites, a gigantic ruin that feeds its contractors—everywhere, but especially on fire walls or walls around villas, which are embedded with broken glass to prevent access and ward off the evil eye, those cakes are drying, and all of them, as though works of art, are signed with three fingerprints.

And so once more, beauty intrudes in some purely utilitarian, ad hoc item. All framed and pedestaled works of art should be forced to compete with such scenes from reality. I saw walls filled with dung cakes that marched in stirring order to the left,

37

to the right, yet leaving space for Calcutta's murals, the hammer and sickle, the Congress hand, and other party symbols— as if tolerating politics.

. . . and whatever the time of day, as if there were no time, old women squat on curbstones and rinse out bottles, or wait, with nothing in their hands, for the day to pass.

The two of us at night, with books under the mosquito net, as if searching for footing on the old fat tomes. Ute knows what comforts her. We have to stay up late, reading *Joseph and His Brothers*, a legend both strangely relevant to India and yet so out of place.

And each evening the pavement dwellers, who, if they have work, are often sweepers in nearby middle-class households, sweep their own spot for sleep on the cracked pavement, the broom—their hallmark—always with them. There they lie, as if sloshed from a bucket.

In a semi-ruin in the Moslem quarter, near the Great Mosque. There, in holes that were once rooms, are quartered six, seven young medical assistants, earning five hundred fifty rupees— less than fifty dollars—a month. They are friendly, ask questions, hardly wait for answers, bring me a chair, a piece of cardboard so I can sketch more comfortably (from the fifth floor) noonday nappers on the roof terraces nearby. The young doctors regret they cannot offer tea; all their water has to be drawn in buckets from a hole on the ground floor.

On every flat roof, in every direction, shops, shacks, family hovels, piles of trash. I count with my pen, as though having to establish a lasting inventory: tin pipes, tires, scrap wood, jute sacks stuffed with paper, baskets, earthen pots, bicycle parts, snarls of wire, bottles being sorted . . .

Later Daud pushes us down side streets and through narrow passages into areas that seem forgotten. Inner courtyards, where men from Orissa—only men—live, they have found work in Calcutta, far away, in place and time, from their families. Then past an Anglican church, waiting in cool classicism for Sundays to come; then through the Armenian cemetery, where among the many gravestones, one declares that long before Job Charnock built his first shed on this accursed spot (and called it Calcutta), Armenian merchants had set up trade.

Later, suddenly, in the midst of this thickly settled decay, we find ourselves standing before a huge, grandiose synagogue, alien and earnest, maintained intact and clean by its remnant congregation. Behind the iron grating of the gate, steps free of weeds lead to the locked temple.

We are moving, no more packed commuter trains for us. From Baruipur to Lake Town on Calcutta's east side. With all our stuff: suitcases, cardboard boxes, and fifteen plastic bags; with ironing board and garbage can, with all our spices and some leftover goulash, with books read—just finished Prem Chand's bitter village tales—and not yet read; with our Bengali household and steamer trunk, abandoning our (deceptive) garden idyll. We are greeted by a power outage, and must put things away by candlelight and immobile fan. Two rooms, a bath, a kitchen. (Imam, the Institute's driver, picked us up in a VW bus.)

Dinner is set out: rice, dhal, fish, chicken, the oversweet sweets. Our host, Shuva's father-in-law, has gathered his family. An excess of kindliness. A desk in the study. The steamer trunk can serve as a standing desk. (Not settled in yet, Ute is still taking her leave of Djanara.)

Lake Town is considered a middle-class enclave, yet is seeped through by festering slums. Here, too, cows pasture on evergrowing mountains of garbage. Middle-class gentility attenuates neighborhood noise, but the noise has moved closer.

After we have established that the bedroom fan is adjustable and have spread ourselves out over the room—my brushes, pens, charcoal, fixative—Ute, as if the move has caused a re-

39

lapse, starts reading Fontane again. I'm on page 1000 in my Joseph novel ("back from quaint Egypt"). Thomas Mann's masterpiece of prestidigitation and bravura, amazing even in its digressions. The reader thinks, He's just showing off. Behold what my mind can conjure up between heaven and earth! And then the author casually picks up the thread of his tale, pushing his legend farther and farther through the desert. And let the nitpickers—always suspicious of craftsmanship—just try it themselves.

Sketches, into the night. Among them, noonday nappers, lying wherever shade falls: diagonal on the pavement, braided into the shafts of rickshas, on the butchering tables of New Market, free-floating on scaffolds, in concrete pipes, under lianaed trees, between other sleepers who seem to have tumbled there.

And today with Daud to see the consul general of Federal Germany. Over ten years ago, a single poem—telling how Mohammed (and other founders of religions) questioned massacres carried out by fanatic believers—put him in prison, in danger for his life, and finally into exile. His bleak story recited for the consul. The mess of papers passed across the desk: applications, refusals, and futile appeals by writers of renown, that Daud Haider at last be granted Indian citizenship. The consular official's advice: he should try once again to get a Bangladesh passport. Only then, after this has been denied, should asylum be requested. . . . (How patient Daud remains, steadfastly amicable, his rage tucked inside.)

Our fourth day without running water. We make do with buckets that have to be hauled a long distance. Escape into sketching. Bearers, how they move under the weight of firewood; so slight and fragile, and yet with such long strides. Hills of garbage under siege by people, crows, and vultures. Against the horizon: an industrial area with a slum encamped before it.

And, everywhere, cows lying diagonal to traffic, arranged

40

beside sleepers, or piled into a landscape of hills. As if, already so distant by intent, I wanted to sketch myself into a greater distance. (My fixative will soon be used up.) As if sketching is an excuse to interrupt these words.

Contrary to all the rules of weather: rain since early this morning. That steady Tagore rain that shapes the lyric poetry of Bengal.

Along with Shuva and Sipra and other guests, we are invited by a literary scholar for cheese and wine. A lengthy exchange about West Bengal and Bangladesh as compared with the division of East and West Germany. The religious difference—here a preponderance of Hindus, there an exclusivity of Moslems, except for a few Hindu enclaves—is more basic than the pasted-on ideological polarity that divides German from German. And likewise, how the religious difference increases the cultural distance—in thought, speech, writing—whereas German culture is separated by nothing more weighty than administrative measures. All this contradicted by the rhetoric of Bengali intellectuals on both sides, who are forever flying the (unifying) flag of their Tagore, and also—in equally blockheaded fashion—the banner of their Netaji. (A little later, during our brief trip to Bangladesh, the mere mention of the Bengali Führer will unleash almost fanatical hymns of allegiance.) What a good thing that at present there is no unifier (living or dead) standing at the German door.

Yesterday we drove with Shuva to the north side of Calcutta, to the statuary quarter, where he is to pick up a Kali, about five feet tall, for his family's puja.

The alley between the sheds is full of divinities, squeezed tightly together in all sizes and styles, with some still unclad, just gray clay. Traffic is jammed, rickshas, other vehicles; atop them, their freight, the terrible goddess. Suddenly, a dispute between bearers and ricksha pullers. Rage, ignited by five ru-

41

pees too few. A flood of words, drama, and farce. And over everything, the carnival-like illumination for the festival. Cannon salutes, firecrackers, brass bands in crazy uniforms and as cacophonous as Schleswig-Holstein's drum and bugle corps.

On the back shelves of the sculptors' sheds, dim in twilight, the leftover gods of festivals past. Lately, we're told, Lakshmi Puja brought luck to the city and its inhabitants. Just before, Durga with her attendants had been an extravagant guest for three days. Everywhere fat Ganesh waves his trunk, rides his rat, while bits of straw stick out of his framework. Not a belly wrinkle, not a flab of fat omitted. The sculptors have the know-how, and apparently the business, too, even though the floods right before Durga Puja caused some losses.

Kali glistens, usually under a layer of black enamel, more rarely of muted blue. Tongue and palms red, and rims around the fixed eyes. Siva, her divine spouse, on whose belly she squats or dances, has to be a pale off-white or piglet pink. Submissive, fat in a female sort of way, he suggests the threatening "Off-with-your-head!" command. Next there's Kali's retinue: women equipped with Dracula teeth, holding child-sized men in their talons, biting off heads, hands, and cocks, balls included. Decorative chains that Kali wears as festive adornment, each link a male head, are for sale, as are other accessories, at shops among the sculptors' stalls. Many of those heads suggest portraits. Businessmen, tea-shop owners, and high-placed bureaucrats from the Writers' Building, their eyes filled with surprise and terror. Shuva's bearded head and my own, mustached, also hang—we try not to notice—as pearls in Kali's necklace.

In the *Telegraph* I read that these several days, during which Kali is exhibited in over a thousand festival tents and at countless family pujas, will also serve as an official commemoration of Indira Gandhi, murdered two years ago. That fits the Black Goddess—sowing daily terror all around her. The reciprocal

42

decapitations in Bihar, where people have been joining up with what's left of the Naxalite movement. The carnage among Gurkhas and Bengalis in and around Darjeeling, where our breakfast tea comes from. It is as if under the sign of Kali they are practicing for the ultimate revolution. Sometimes it is the heads of landless farmers, sometimes you see, in news photos, a row of heads from the many-headed family of some rich landowner. (People do not like to talk about the Naxalite revolts of the late sixties, when neither Congress nor Communists held power; Kali alone was in season.)

In the meantime the goddess, purchased the day before, has been set up on her altar in the common room used by our host's extended family. The room, adjacent to our two, is usually furnished only with upholstered benches and an upholstered rocker. All fussily arranged by Shuva (director and chief electrician) and his sisters-in-law, just as with us at home when the crèche is set up and the tree burdened by ornaments and lights. It all looks perfectly peaceful; reconciliation with Kali. A Brahman is promised for the ceremonies once the festival gets into high gear.

And they do this year in, year out: routine activity. But the evening bustle in the street markets, a few of them illegal, has something mystical about it, when candles and guttering oil and kerosene lamps are the only illumination, and the heads of customers, as they hesitate or move on, already belong to the darkness heavy with smoke. Lots of black ink will be needed to capture such scenes, in which Kali goes haunting.

Into the Chinese quarter, surrounded by walls that are penetrable thanks solely to Daud's skill, in the northeast of the city, on the way to the Garbage Mountains of Dhapa, whose stench blends with the fumes of the leather factories and tanneries, all of them the property of the Chinese. Here there is no trace of the noise and pageantry of the beginning Kali Puja. The workers in the factories are Moslems from Bihar, now the coolies of the same Chinese who in the nineteenth century were brought in as coolies by the English. Only Hindus of no caste would ever accept work as tanners.

The Chinese live apart. It proves difficult to engage them in conversation. Courteous mistrust persists. They maintain several schools, kindergartens, newspapers. During the Sino-Indian War of 1962 they were under supervision, their movements restricted. Even today they are not secure from expatriation. Some of the older Chinese returned to the motherland. Many emigrated to Canada, to Europe. Within their ghetto, an unusual scene for Calcutta: young women and girls on mopeds.

But the Chinese quarter in the center of the city is wretched, squeezed. Daud leads us across slippery steps into four-story hovels. One family per room, the family workshop in the same room: noodle production. A goat on the fourth floor. Tea is offered at once. A man of extreme old age (from Nanking) is about to return home. But here, too, a school is maintained. For each child attending school, the parents pay six rupees a month. The school, its courtyard cleanly swept—amid piles of trash and an omnipresent stench (leather manufacture, the sale of dried fish)—was founded by a Chinese factory owner. Even after the end of the school day, the empty classrooms convey the discipline of daily routine, as does the old teacher as he shows us the student notebooks. Every student, from age five on, learns to speak and write Chinese, English, Hindi, and Bengali. (One is tempted to ask why the Indians, after so many lessons learned from the English, have no desire to learn from the Chinese?)

As we are trying to find a taxi after our South Indian dinner (vegetarian), the streets are still jammed all the way to the suburbs. Wedged into the throng, you must pay close attention to each step you take on the creviced streets and sidewalks. We

44

are never close together, always just barely in each other's view, and yet we don't get lost.

So this is Kali Puja! From early evening until shortly before midnight, the priest—a young Brahman teacher who has been fasting since yesterday—works with flowers and garlands and bowls filled with vegetarian food. Hangs them on Kali, places them around her, pelts her with them, until the Black Goddess, already bordered about with Shuva's colorful still lifes, is drowning in delights. The chain of hacked-off male heads, her firm stance atop Siva's belly, and her tongue—the proof of her shame—can only be surmised.

Everything is left to the priest. Toward the end, elderly women, some out loud, some only muttering, join his litanies. Otherwise, while he purrs mantras and tosses flowers according to strict canons, the small talk goes on among the extended family, themselves half-and-half believers, and the arriving and departing guests. The children play games behind the Brahman's back, unreprimanded by their mothers.

After a good two hours of prayer, which works the priest into a sweat—the fan fails from time to time as well—incense is burned, cymbals banged, one of the old women blows on a conch to the tinkle of bells, while outside the noise increases, now with thunderclaps nearby and rockets ascending in all colors. The mothers stuff cotton balls into the ears of the smaller children.

I hold out until the consecrated food is eaten. An exhausted Ute has fallen asleep, her book at her side. Only the men squat and eat from banana leaves, using one deft hand, then the other. The Brahman manages to put away a large amount of rice and dhal, dhal and rice. A normal feed, wordless and efficient. Of Kali, whom I am trying to comprehend—"Our mad mother," one prayer says, "who takes and gives, gives and takes"—there's not a trace. And yet, in what Christian church, no matter among which faction of believers, can the presence of the radical

Jesus of Nazareth be conclusively shown? (No, there is no reason to concede any mitigating circumstances to religions, however pious the swindle they offer.)

I spend the afternoon drawing people in garbage. Since the brief dusk, which abruptly turned into night, noise again everywhere—bangs, and now, the laments of trumpeted conch shells. I go with Shuva and his wife (carrying a bouquet from his sisters-in-law) to the movies, to see a Hindi film: *Friends, Enemies*. The director's name is Rao, a favorite in Krishna roles and the prime minister of an Indian federal state as well. We walk to the movie palace in the center of Lake Town, near the water tower that dominates all else.

What we see is a cleverly brewed melodrama, interrupted every ten minutes by song and dance numbers or stylized acrobatic fisticuffs. The language: Hindi larded with English. The audience reacts as if it were a Western. Loud outrage whenever the picture or sound grows dim or fails completely for several minutes. To reality—to whatever extent the facts in this film are real—no semblance. In the film a police inspector, who in actuality earns a thousand rupees a month, barely eighty dollars, lives in a brand-new luxury apartment. And this, without being, as national custom dictates, corrupt. Naturally, the ending reveals that the woman, who as pickpocket and beggar has been responsible for all the episodes of commotion, is not an Untouchable, but comes, rather, from the best of families. In Indian dreams, too, the world—if only for the duration of a film—must be whole.

We are barely out of the theater, and the other film knocks us flat: the extravagant racket in honor of the Black Goddess.

He sketches, makes notes; she silently counts the days. He wants to maintain the distance he's won, to enlarge it; she is at the Jewish bakery (hidden in New Market) in search of an approximation of the black bread of home. He asks to hear

46

(taking pains to be patient) the names of her everchanging ailments; when necessary (and in secret), she consults her trained apothecary. He settles in; she holds out.

Weight loss, followed by atrophy of muscles. After three months, Calcutta begins to gnaw. Yet the sketching and recording do not abate, even when eyes have grown tired and dry from all the openly spread-out misery. She writes letters. The first draft of his poem in twelve cantos is completed. Their common ritual: while she boils water—every day, at least six quarts have to bubble for twenty minutes—he organizes addenda, addenda that call forth further addenda. . . .

Yesterday, late, when driving home through streets lit only haphazardly, a greater number of sleepers. Or is it just that we, our eyes trained now, see them everywhere? Many are hard to spot, lying by walls, in niches. Unlike the sleepers filed head to the wall, in family rows. And then there are the pavement dwellers camped along the median strips of the main streets, in and next to tents of black plastic. Until late at night, we see women cooking over cow-dung fires, hanging out wash. The phrase "a place of one's own" suggests itself. The traffic passing in both directions circumvents the island dwellers.

Resolutions in the sleepless night. Once back in Germany, measure everything, myself included, by Calcutta. Stick to the topic, black on black. Publicly, nothing but what I've written, drawn. (At most, battle for two, three percent at election time.) Resolutions . . .

Suddenly, in the midst of a maze of alleys, behind the columnlike facade of palm trees, surprised by the sight of a palatial edifice. Along with Daud, into the Marble Palace, which is packed with European curios and big daubs in oil, covered by layer upon layer of varnish—among them there is said to be a genuine Rubens (but which one is it?)—and takes its name from the floors and walls inlaid with slabs of one hundred and six

47

different kinds of marble. Copies of Greek and Roman sculptures, tons, best measured by the shipload. Venetian candelabra and breathless rococo clocks. Vases, with and without cracks. Visible from all angles, a double-chinned Queen Victoria, larger than life, carved in ebony down to the last pleat of her skirt. We pass barefoot through suites of rooms.

On the top floor, dusky furniture under plastic covers. I count four Napoleons in bronze. Apart from mournful parrots who reside in shit-laden cages placed around the galleries of the inner court, the only living things are three or four guards in khaki, knickered and putteed, and one other person: a Mullick, of the Mullick family of former days, running around the gallery from parrot to parrot. His greasy naked torso gleams above his loincloth, called a dhoti. His bald head, too, glistens with fat, as if marked for Kali's sickle.

Together with his family, this Mullick occupies the top floor of one wing in the Marble Palace and is himself, as he runs back and forth, part of the exhibit. We're told he employs over two hundred people and that (obedient to an oath once sworn by the Mullicks during a famine) he feeds three hundred of the poor every day. Later we see the poor squatting in long rows under trees at the edge of the park; before them, rice and mashed yellow lentils on banana leaves, more handout than idyll.

In the park, red deer are fed, as is a six-foot snake whose bivouac is a basket trunk. The young man (also an employee of the Mullick) who opens the trunk lid a crack for us, tells of a daily snake ration of one pigeon. With no transition, slum abuts the park's borders.

Later we visit the palace of another Mullick, who lives off his leased estates, is an amateur poet, maintains a library, and every two months invites guests for literary events in the palace courtyard enclosed by delicate wrought-iron grating. (From every angle you immediately see a good shot for a movie.) In the palace interior: gloom broken by aisles of light. Chandeliers of Bohemian crystal (intended for candles) hang inside plastic

48

bags. All the paintings blackened. Dust on glasses and figurines. The mirrors dead, as if turned to the wall.

Along the gallery are poorly framed miniatures of northern India, magnanimously exposed to decay, already ruined by water spots and mold. The master of the house uses a flashlight, likewise sheathed in plastic, as if needing the same protection as the chandeliers, to show us village scenes delicately traced in a Persian tapestry. And then the silver throne of the family god, said to come from Orissa.

The family arrives for tea: all the ladies of the house, a fidgety nephew. We are shown the few occupied rooms, sparely, haphazardly furnished. Then we climb to the roof; several layers of terraces. In the twilight, by full moon, the smoke of the crematoriums approaches in soft strokes from the river and daubs at the black of the courtyards. My unbidden love for this city, a city damned to offer lodgings to every human misery. I want to return here and draw—but from the roof.

Later we eat with Armata Sankara Ray and his Lila, who have taken Daud in and treat him like a son. When Ray was young, he sat at Gandhi's feet. With a smile, the eighty-five-year-old man shows us the fourth and last volume of his memoirs.

At home, I draw what I have sketched of a morning: a small slum clustered about a monument pedestal; atop the monument, a bust of stone . . .

Since yesterday, the Moslem slum, to the right of the approach ramp to the bridge bypass, is decked out in bright pennants in honor of Mohammed's birthday.

It has been raining, the storm winds increasing, since four this morning. A typhoon over the Bay of Bengal, moving toward Orissa, is allegedly to blame. Anger at the mere thought of the mostly low-lying slums. I can no longer respond politely to thoughtless, friendly questions about how we're doing in Calcutta. The arrangements for our trip to Santiniketan are firm.

49

An academic idyll awaits us. The enthusiasm of intellectuals for Tagore's university is all too unanimous. It is quiet there, peaceful, they say, and so on. There, you feel as if you're outside the world. There, you have leisure time. Only a few speak ironically of Tagore's "lost paradise."

As Shuva drives us at five o'clock to Howrah Station in his father-in-law's car, the streets, whole sections of the city are still knee-deep in water. We see fringe slums battered by the wind, the tentlike caves of the pavement dwellers. Skinny figures wrapped in blankets seek refuge along house walls and on high-ground curbs. Coolies shove heavy-laden two-wheel carts through the flooded streets. Stranded cars, their motors drowned, block traffic. All the same we arrive at Howrah Station on time, only to discover that the six o'clock train to Santiniketan does not run on Sundays. So, tickets for the local train that departs in just under an hour. Shuva supplies bits of advice.

In the booking hall, on the platforms, everywhere, they lie, wrapped in thin blankets, on the concrete, some on bast mats. Several children under one blanket. On their sides, drawn up, women sheltering tiny bundles between breast and crook of the arm. Since they all are lying in loosely arranged rows, it is easy to get through. Where someone lies athwart, we step over.

A ticket costs eleven rupees. The train has only one class. Through windows with no panes, the cool draft of motion and morning pours in. A historian, to whom Shuva introduced us on the platform, plans to give a lecture at Santiniketan; later he will help us find a place to stay.

Our conversation skips in the draft between his curiosity and mine. He is interested in the positions Adenauer and Schumacher (centrist and socialist) took in the late forties and early fifties; I want him to explain the diffuse Bengali longing for a Führer figure and also why, at the same time, Gandhi's ideas are neglected. The partitions of Germany and Bengal. The English, he says, once they got a toehold on the subcontinent,

50

had found a long-established system of control and exploitation, which they took over, then expanded in the days of Clive and Hastings, used modern forms of tax collection, and—once they had thoroughly plundered the vast colony—passed the system on to the ruling (still ruling) Congress Party. Gandhi's demands—land reform, elementary education, development of the villages, protection for tribes of aboriginal inhabitants, equality for the Untouchables—was never, or only rudimentarily, realized, not to mention his postulate of nonviolence. India had neglected to find a path of its own, and was now in danger of falling apart, politically and socially. The middle and upper classes—barely a quarter of the population—were trying very hard to write off the rest. . . .

During our exchange, vendors, sellers of lottery tickets, beggars, and singers pass through the train. To the tune of their plucked instruments, the singers recite poems that can be bought by the single sheet or in brochures. And there are buyers, because the Bengalis live not by rice, fish, dhal, and oversweet pastries alone, but by lyric poetry as well.

In Santiniketan we find lodging at the guest house of Tagore University. After the noon meal (mutton, dhal, rice), the director of the university takes us on a tour of the buildings erected by Tagore and his son. Only the mud-walled one leaves any impression, although its ornamented facade—relief made of a blend of clay, loam, sand, and cow dung—is greasy with black tar and rather dreadful.

Why do museums do such violence to the people they exhibit? The surfeit of photos shows Tagore as a picture-book guru swollen with dignity; Gerhart Hauptmann in half-profile comes to mind. All of them, including the director, speak solemnly when speaking of Rabindranath Tagore. Only later, outside the museum, as the director tells us of the twenty-two-year-old poet's marriage to a child and of his unhappy love for Indira Devi, his brother's wife, does the poet become human. Indira Devi chose a nine-year-old girl to be her lover's bride;

51

then, four months after the wedding, she committed suicide. The girl, once she was a woman and had borne a sufficient number of children, died young.

On the university grounds, we are impressed by amphitheaters for instruction under the collective shade of old trees. All these charming daughters and petal-white sons, assembled in a circle around their teacher, mock the misery of India. Here, too, the preferred subject of instruction is nineteenth-century English literature. Tagore, however, had wanted to promote the many languages of India. Unfortunately, the director says, the courses for Marathi, Tamil, Urdu, etc., have few takers. (While I draw, Ute sits off to one side—alone with her thoughts under what distant pear tree?)

The next day, we visit two Santal villages, the first on the edge of the university grounds, the other, two miles distant in a glade of young eucalypti, a new planting in land where the soil is stripped almost bare to the rock. In both villages, roomy mud-wall buildings often arranged in a square around a farmyard. No piles of garbage, no overgrown rubble, no potholes, no off-to-the-side place for Untouchables. In each farmyard, cows, goats, chickens, and pigeons. For the pigeons, dovecotes made of earthenware jars hung from the rice-straw roofs. The Santals are a tribal people older even than the Dravidians of southern India. Compared with Hinduism, their religion of animism seems almost reasonable. They eat any kind of meat. The bride does not have to be made acceptable to the groom and his family with a dowry and a moped thrown into the bargain. Divorces are possible. It's rumored that they even practice birth control (a well-kept secret). An average of three to four children per Santal family, five or more among Hindu farmers. In the first village (near the university) there are mixed marriages. The Santals, both men and women, regularly drink a schnapps distilled from rice and other fermented vegetable matter. It seems to do them good. A woman pulls away a cloth

52

covering brimming basins, the fuel of village intoxications. With a laugh she tells of drinking habits.

In the first village, the majority vote Communist (CPI)M. Above the alms box in the village center a graffito reads: Vote Communist! Even the village priest is elected and can be removed from office. An ancient Santal, his white beard falling to his loincloth, shows us a patchwork umbrella he has sewn and then embroidered with a pictographic history of his tribe.

In the wooded village, the university director talks about efforts made on behalf of the Santals. The well here was built by a former supporter of the Naxalites, who, after the uprisings came to their bloody end (and after some time in the underground), found his way to Gandhi's ideas and now wants to use his organization to revive Tagore's reforms. . . .

Various reliefs of animals are projected in almost full form from the mud walls; their bulging bases are edged with stripes of pink or blue. We watch women stirring a loamy brew. Now that the monsoons are over, the cracks and eroded holes in the walls will be repaired.

The next day we visit the university's model farm and several craft workshops. Only vestiges of Tagore's reforms can be seen. The farmyard is filthy, the chicken farm a factory using fishmeal feed. A bull, at least, stands still while I sketch. (He is only seldom put to use, we're told. They lack pastureland for any real breeding.)

Among the weavers, only four looms are operating. A good dozen more are ruined, abandoned, dusty, hardly recognizable as looms. No one in the surrounding villages wants to learn the craft, because when they complete the course, they have no means to set up a weaving business of their own.

The pottery is disheartening, the leatherwork inferior. Only the papermakers deliver a presentable product—sheets in various sizes. I buy ten, for subjects that lie on the streets of Calcutta.

53

An evening walk through the town of Santiniketan, where we drink tea in various cookshops and chew the sad cud of so many futile efforts. Back at our guest house we run into two Russians. Both are visiting lecturers at the university: she a language teacher, he an engineer. We drink beer that the director has considerately arranged to have brought to us. Far from our home continent, we speak not as Federal Germans and Soviet citizens, but rather as Europeans equally dismayed by India's realities. Ute perks up; the language teacher, from Riga, assures her that the Baltic is still making little waves. (With the last swallow we toast Gorbachev, worried that his reforms could be wrecked by inertia and become no more than memorial ruins, like Gandhi's ideas, like Tagore's experiment. . . .)

In the early train to Calcutta, we again hear singers reciting poems to the tune of their one-stringed instruments. One boy with a braying voice has particular success. Many of our Bengali fellow passengers wag their heads—it looks like disapproval—in approval.

Hardly have I returned from Santiniketan, and I hear the complaints of Bengali writers. The "Indian Week" during the Frankfurt Book Fair was a fraud. Invited and trotted out, they had merely been used for show. Some splendid art books were sold, yes, but no large publishing house was seriously interested in the literatures of India.

I am shamed by these complaints, not merely because they are justified. Whether in Berlin, Hamburg, or Frankfurt, people like to deck themselves out with "Third World" exhibitionism, are willing to pay a pretty penny for a raree-show, and that includes the Association of German Book Dealers. A few hundred thousand marks are quickly freed up; competent managers, bursting with ideas for scenic backdrops, can always be found. It fits right in with the international festival setting. Something always has to be happening, as garish, as exotic as

54

possible, with just a touch of political involvement. Yet if you were to suggest that these freed-up funds be invested instead in literary translations from the languages of India, the curtain would fall with a thud. Not impressive enough. Small beer. Too low-key and offbeat for the media, and far too far away. . . .

Later, at the Institute, a short film by Mrynal Sen. A Communist functionary, now that his party is in power, sees to it that he and his wife are taken care of: a largish apartment, new furniture, a telephone. And the wife, who has been working as a rural teacher, is likewise offered a position in the city (Calcutta). We watch an accurate study of everyday corruption and its strange consequence: the conversation by night between the functionary and his wife about their great loss amid their small gains, the shame . . .

On the drive from the Institute to Lake Town—beneath a spreading tree, three slum tents in the shadows. Children playing marbles in the garbage, the unemployed squatting on heaps of gravel. In Lake Town, my ten sheets of paper have arrived, twelve rupees a sheet.

Daud and his friend Sourav pick us up. We drive to Paturia Ghat Street, to visit the Mullick (and poet) in whose gloomy palace Fellini could make a film: *The Return of Netaji*. . . .

From the palace roof I sketch the city, excited because I'm new to such vistas. Then on to the nearby crematorium that—like the slum along the railroad tracks—we have seen once before. The Mullick, whose family once owned what is today a publicly owned facility for bathing and cremation, accompanies us. Several ghat employees abandon their pyres to watch as I draw.

Three fires are burning; one has burned low, the corpse turned to ashes. Down toward the Ganges, the courtyard opens to scenery through which pass thinning swathes of smoke. Simultaneously, the chant of young men around a new fire,

55

and the forsaken corpses once the cremation draws to an end. Occasionally someone adds wood or shoves a charred piece— is it a body part or a branch?—back into the blaze. The slightly sweet odor. Hollows in the ripped brick pavement of the courtyard; the pavement free now for more corpses. Walls, smoke-black, thick with inscriptions, black on black, name on name.

As we walk past the large pile of lumber on our way back to the palace, the Mullick explains cremation customs to us. The oldest or youngest son must walk several times around his father's corpse bedded on the wood, reciting prayers, then thrust a flaming chip in the open mouth, then finally ignite the fire.

That evening in Alipore, where Messrs. Consuls (*avec mesdames*) dwell as neighbors with the nouveaux riches, we hear Carl Orff's *Carmina Burana*, music that, with the aid of soloists, chorus, and orchestra, strives to behave barbarously. "La Martinière," the college for the upper and upper-middle classes, and the director of the Institute (Max Mueller Bhavan), who would have done better to be conductor in Kiel, Bonn, or wherever, are in charge of the open-air pomp. (For special sound effects, four extra instrumentalists have been flown in.) A lost, obscene evening. During the drive home: reflections on pyres, sleepers in shadows, vigilant cows . . .

She reads as if on the sly. To fight fever, nausea, inflammations, homesickness, and dizzy spells now, too—she takes her antidote. He varies his dream. It was not he who met her by accident, taking control, but rather she who has bought, at just the right moment, a little (thatch-roofed) house on the Baltic coast of Holstein, paying too much for it, so that she can live there with her children, until one day a coach-and-two drives by, its passenger a gentleman in his mid-sixties, who introduces himself and at once, no sooner does he set foot in the parlor, requests a quiet room facing the sea, full board—a respectable love affair that leaves me out. Add a garden behind the cottage,

56

ready to offer a pear tree with shade enough for three or four (in case his Emilie should follow him) and far enough from Calcutta, where everything presents itself in garish light and inflames Ute's eyes.

Smog weighs on the city once the monsoon downpours are over. With Daud, Sourav, and Tripaty to the theater, the one across from the Maidan, where open markets are held and throngs of people are gathering.

The play concerns a thief who uses native wit to rob, one after the other, a guru, a rich landowner (zamindar), a portly Brahman. Each time, tweaking a policeman's nose. Naturally the thief steals only for the poor, for which the common people love him. But then, after he has pocketed the crown jewels (in their velvet casket) of a sovereign princess and pulled several tricks on the corrupt police chief, he is finally nabbed and brought before the princess. She takes a shine to him, but not he to her. Despite his hunger, he rejects her food, her love, and finally is handed over to soldiers, who put him to an impressive death.

The actors, the singers who comment on the action from downstage like old-fashioned balladeers (so that we, too, understand), are all amateurs from a remote village, performing here only after their harvest, and all are members of a tribe that belongs to India's aboriginal population (a despised minority). The acrobatic thief, the expressive balladeers, the dancing in the interludes, all of it, all of them, provide amusement, particularly since Habib Tanvir, the play's director, manages to slip in, very casually, the scandals of the hour. (Astonishing, the sparse applause from an audience that has been enthralled for two hours.)

Afterward, we eat in a vegetarian restaurant. Even this late, seemingly aimless crowds move about. That day, over four hundred thousand had assembled on the Maidan to participate in the Left-Front government's celebration of the beginning election campaign. Many supporters of the CPI(M) were brought into the city by truck, paid a day's wages. Others, here since yesterday, had to spend the night in the open. (To us it seems as though the play were continuing in the open, as though the acrobatic thief might suddenly make his entrance again, only this time to tweak the noses of Party functionaries, unmask the parliamentarians, and torpedo the latest corrupt scheme.)

It is cooler at night now. We too lie under blankets. Using yesterday's sketches, I work till late in the evening, drawing a slum that sprang up as if overnight, propped in single file against a factory wall. Once again the (unwritten) aesthetics of poverty shocks me: how every detail of the huts made of rags, sheets of plastic, cardboard, and jute sacks, is so terribly palpable, cries out for a name. This ultimate beauty challenges every other canon of beauty.

Before our trip to Bangladesh—where Daud's fourteen brothers and sisters await us—I want to capture faces: the resigned anxiety, the concentrated gravity of those squatters who, because they no longer work, no longer have anything to wait for. How faceless the middle class is, how soon its people run to fat. Everything I have to show, proves only that I've been observant, nothing more.

In the night, late, I get caught up in reading a thin volume by Gour Kishore Ghosh, *Let Me Have My Say*, written during Indira Gandhi's reign of terror and protesting equally the systematic executions carried out by the Naxalites. A democrat hopelessly between two fronts . . .

At the security gate—we have only a half-hour flight ahead of us—one of the customs officers casually swipes two cigars from my case: he is fond of Brazilian cigars. We failed to apply officially for our departure and return. I make up for our failure, in writing, but our residency permits for India remain with the

58

airport police all the same. This misappropriation will have bureaucratic consequences up to our departure for Europe.

Six million people in a provincial city, the capital of a state about twice the size of Bavaria but with over a hundred million inhabitants, their number growing at an annual rate of three percent. Only twenty percent can read and write. Neither the massacres of 1946–47 nor the decimation of 1971, when Bangladesh became independent, have improved the statistics; nor, for that matter, have the routine floods with their subsequent epidemics.

Fewer cars than in Calcutta, but a hundred thousand licensed bicycle rickshas. The air is better, less garbage in the streets, no cows blocking traffic. And the wide arteries into the city, broad for military parades, are free of potholes.

A group of writers receives us with flowers at the Dacca airport. After a meal (Chinese), we sleep without mosquito nets and feel naked. The next morning, off to the old city in a brightly painted ricksha. It takes a while to strike a bargain for the price. Belal Chowdhury, a writer, is our guide.

In this Moslem city, the street scene is dominated by men, except in one section where Hindus live as a minority. Like Daud, Belal leads us with no fuss into workshops, introduces us to families. A young man, in his very narrow quarters enlarged by plank sheds, opens up the secret house altar hidden in a cupboardlike chest: Durga, Ganesh, Lakshmi amid bric-a-brac, plus a doll's bed with mosquito net, in which the divinities are placed when it's time for sleep. The fear of new pogroms is denied with a smile—hardly worth their while. A family with many children.

Then workshops where iron blades are used to saw seashells into bracelets. The left foot presses the shell against a wooden block, the saw is placed right next to the toes and operated with both hands. Despite the metal blade, a stone-age production method. Later we visit the remains of the vast Lal Bagh fortress from the era of the Moguls. A rather meager museum at least demonstrates how painstakingly the English, zealots for culture, went about enriching their own museums—comparable to Greater Germany's Field Marshal Göring and his love for the artistic treasures of foreign nations.

That afternoon, a discussion at the university about the systematic extermination of the tribal population in the Chittagong highlands: Bengali racism knows no national boundaries. Within Bangladesh, the military government does not allow public criticism of its annihilation campaign. But the opposition, elected by the middle class, is little concerned about the fate of the "tribals." Here too (as in Calcutta), the daily struggle to stay alive absorbs every sympathy that might extend beyond one's own family, one's own group.

An invitation, which Belal declines, and for good reason— a dinner with other writers at the home of an industrialist reputed to be a lover of literature. His wife at once delivers two Tagore songs in a smoky voice accompanied by a harmonium. During the meal, the conversation tosses out questions that seldom wait for answers. Amid political allusions, enjoyed around the table for their wit, we get down to the main topic. Although Bengal is divided for good and all, and for that reason alone is comparable to Germany, the admiration expressed for Subhas Chandra Bose is undivided, permits no doubts.

The next day, to the potters, who will soon be out of work, since plastic dishes are increasingly dominating the market. Behind the potters' settlement, a wide river landscape. On a peninsula are camped river gypsies, who deal in snakes, shells, medicinal herbs. In the foreground, a ship is being unloaded. The multiple mouths of the Ganges, interconnected, transport in all directions freight by sailboat and people by steamer. Several boats deliver river sludge, which the potters mix with their clay. Here too, piles of firewood, weighing scales beside them.

In the afternoon, Belal takes us to Geneva Camp, a sprawling and overcrowded slum where twenty thousand Moslem Biharis are encamped. In 1947, they tried to emigrate from the Indian state of Bihar to West Pakistan, but were shunted to East Pakistan. Many of the men found work with the railroad. When East Pakistan, with India's military assistance and after a long period of butchery, became Bangladesh, the Biharis again chose Pakistan, but that affection was not reciprocated and they had to remain here, the door back to India, to Bihar, closed to them. Bangladesh treats them as displaced persons: an insufficient supply of water, restricting work permits, no public health services. With a constant shortage of rice, eighty percent of the children are undernourished.

The Pakistan-Biharis are not recognized as refugees by the United Nations. The Red Cross in Geneva passed the problem to its Bangladesh branch, which in turn passed it to the municipal authorities in Dacca. So that no one does anything, except for a few Christian relief agencies, who occasionally deliver rice. (From other Islamic states all that has arrived, so far, are bundles of propaganda.)

There is a small school, used by two thousand children in three shifts. Out of families with six to eight children, often only one child is allowed to attend the school. Along with Urdu and Bengali, English is taught. Upon graduation, the student must pay the state examiners a fee of six hundred takas, about what a teacher earns in a month.

Geneva Camp is one slum among many. Over two hundred thousand Biharis, who cannot move to Pakistan, live in such camps, which are slums. Recently one of these slums burned down. No water to extinguish the fire, many deaths. When I speak to politicians about the misery in Geneva Camp, they respond: A tragedy. And change the subject. (I wonder if, when I get back to Berlin, I would have any success organizing some help—if only for the school?) As if by way of an apology, Belal says that until now he, too, has seen this slum only from the outside. . . .

At five in the morning, off to the country. In the fresh morning air, freezing figures wrapped in cloths, shawls, blankets. Most of the huts have tin roofs. The countryside is more thickly settled than in West Bengal. Village merges into village. Our destination is a muslin market in Tangail. In the press of people, the displayed rolls of fabric can barely be seen. But who, except the middlemen who control the market, can buy these airy webs?

Afterward, we visit nearby Pathrail, a weaver village where Hindus live, about seven thousand of them. Silence, only the clatter of looms. For eleven days, a weaver sits bent over a sari, which will bring him one thousand takas, about thirty dollars. The dependence on middlemen will soon force the weavers to give up and emigrate to Bengal, where middlemen likewise control the market.

Along all the village lanes, threads of unspooled cotton glisten like fresh dew. Cows under the many-branched trees. We walk to the river. So many, many children. Two mongooses playing in the rice field. Recollections of schoolbooks: Rikki-Tikki-Tavi . . .

In comparison to West Bengal, everything here seems more organized, state-controlled. A dictatorship challenged only by graffiti (often painted over) on the university grounds. The president is a general who writes poetry. As if unthreatened, parceled out between arms of the river, this unhappy land lies wide open, up for grabs. The military rules, but there is room for Islam to rule, too, and for western capital. Forty percent of the basic foodstuffs has to be imported. (I ask Daud's family if he would be in danger in the event of his return. A superfluous question. Later, with family members alternating at our side, we are photographed for the album.)

A short drive brings us to a country town with a bloody history, evidenced by ruins and abandoned Hindu temples.

62

Here, too, weavers once lived; the muslin they wove was in great demand, far and wide. To protect the English textile industry, their nimble fingertips were hacked off. Later, Moslems slaughtered the weavers' descendants; the survivors fled. What remains are idyllic, overgrown ruins amid a lush landscape. A tourist center is in the planning stages, to be built next to the museum.

Then more programmed events, roundtable discussions, where the ambitious middle class sets the tone. We slip in a brief visit to Dacca's National Museum. A cavalcade of paintings by Indian-European moderns. Only the brush drawings of Zainul Abedin leave a lasting impression. He was an eyewitness to the Bengali famine of 1943, when over two million Bengalis perished, starving under British rule. If you ask now who was to blame then, you get the usual disagreement over jurisdictions—it was London, it was New Delhi, it was the local authorities—and the cynical recital of hands-tying circumstances: the state of war, the lack of transportation, rivalries among Indians, a bad harvest, the weather, and so on. (By the way, Subhas Chandra Bose, by then under Japanese protection, made a futile offer of hundreds of thousands of tons of Burmese rice. But London would take nothing from its foe.)

Abedin's drawings—on paper beige to reddish-brown, about thirty in all—show beggars, people dying of starvation. A few strokes of the brush, outlines, economical detail. Backgrounds often mere hints. The gestures of hunger, crows atop the dying and the dead, roving dogs. The swollen bellies of the children, the empty bowls, garbage. Often just abbreviations whisked by the almost dry brush.

In later years, Abedin stylized Indian folklore to the point of easiness on the eye. A mural, its subject the aftermath of a hurricane in November, 1970, which in Bangladesh alone swept more than three hundred thousand people into the sea or buried them in mud. The effect purely decorative, although some detail work does recall the early brush drawings.

Driving to the airport—many army units on the move, practicing for the parades. Security precautions for upcoming Independence Day.

The common Bengali names: Mitra, Gupta, Dasgupta, Sen, Dutta, Chowdhury, Ray, Banerjee, Chatterjee, Mukherjee, Basu, Chakrabarty or sometimes Chackerbutty, Bose, like our Subhas Chandra on horseback, Ghose, Ghosh, and, of course, Tagore. Great, widespread names, once (and sometimes even now) synonymous with estates, coal mines, jute mills, dockyards, and wealth—until about a hundred years ago, when the Marwaris, members of a merchant caste from Rajasthan, arrived and, as their numbers and their profits from trading and moneylending increased, grew prosperous enough to buy into real estate and the jute industry.

By the time of the ghee scandal during the First World War (ghee is the holy butter used in religious rites, cremation for instance, and it was being adulterated with beef tallow by the ghee merchants, many of them Marwaris), the dealings of the Marwaris began to draw contempt and hatred, and not just the usual envy. No wonder, for the estates of the Mitras, Mukherjees, and Guptas now belonged to them. They owned the coal mines that had once been the property of the Tagores and Chowdhurys. And when the English, having sucked the subcontinent dry, withdrew their money from Calcutta, the Marwaris jumped in to fill the financial gap. Today, so say Mr. Sen and Mr. Chackerbutty, they own everything, have their hands in everything, nothing happens without them. Birla, for example, with his conglomerate . . .

We are the guests of the wife of a Marwari; her husband, as always, is away on business. Behind high walls, the mansion. Suites of rooms, low-voiced servants, comfortable furniture that might have been borrowed from a television family series. The wife of the Marwari and her girlfriend (who is a Bengali) want to talk about literature; her husband, like all Marwaris,

64

has no interest in such things. And so we chat about her literary agency, which, she candidly admits, is financed by her husband. He is, the friend assures us, a magnanimous and tolerant man.

Rarely have I been more curious about an absent husband. Then he arrives, and wants to know who these guests of his dear wife are. As if basic issues must be addressed at once, he complains—seasoning the complaint with an ironic smile—about the unjustifiably bad reputation of the Marwaris. Pointing to his wife's Bengali friend, he assures us that he is a friend of her husband as well. Unfortunately, however, he will shortly have to buy out the man's jute mill, at his request, because it is on the verge of bankrupcy. A lack of good management. The Bengalis have no sense of reality. A school of management for young, ambitious Bengalis has been established, financed by Marwaris, but with paltry results. One bust after the other. And now people will hate him because he will have to buy yet another jute mill. Of course, it is never the Bengalis' fault, it's always the greedy Marwaris.

This reminds me, I tell him, of German prejudices and their consequences. He supposes that every society, if it has no Jews handy, must invent its Jews. In other places the Jews might be Armenians, Chinese—or Marwaris.

The two women listen silently. He adds that things won't get that bad here. And then, at his request—he doesn't want to interrupt—more literary small talk.

. . . a spot where the three of us—if not under a pear tree at home, then beneath the trees of the Maidan, near the ruins of Fort William, which still function as a barracks for the army—can discuss The Great Indian Mutiny, the sepoy uprising in Bengal and elsewhere. Seen from his point of view, of course.

1857. For more than a year now, Fontane, the press attaché from the Prussian embassy (serving the reactionary Manteuffel military cabinet) has been living in London as the correspondent of the *Kreuz-Zeitung*. He associates little with German émigrés,

65

who suspect him of being a government cat's-paw or even a spy, but has many English contacts. Occasionally he writes for the *Times* and—duty-bound to his employer—bribes the publisher of the *Morning Chronicle* to keep him from printing articles with an anti-Prussian slant. The bribe is an annual payment of two thousand talers.

All of which doesn't sit well with Fontane. Things hardly improve when, in the summer of 1857, Emilie and the children arrive and take up residence in Camden, a suburb in north London.

Fontane's wife finds her husband distraught, his nerves shattered. It may be that besides the ambiguity of his professional situation, yet another problem has added to his imbalance. The Sepoy Mutiny in May of that year, quickly put down by retaliating British troops, has damaged his previously tidy view of England. The Empire's policy in China, which he termed "opium trade and Times logic" in a *Kreuz-Zeitung* report, had previously outraged him. When this time, however, after the butchery following the Mutiny (mutineers were tied to the mouths of cannons) British greed for power reached out and annexed the area under the control of the East India Company in the guise of a crown colony, Fontane reacts with disgust to this excess of Christian cant, naked lust for money, the maxim of "Cotton or Death." He takes ill, demands an extended vacation in the Riesengebirge, which the Manteuffel military cabinet turns down.

So he went to Scotland, old Fontane tells us under the dusty trees of the Maidan. After several digressions up the major and minor valleys of Scotland—and he calls each castle and each clan by name—he picks up his vexing theme once more. Calcutta, you know, got off easy in the Sepoy Mutiny, thanks to its Scottish regiment. The mutinying companies in Barrackpore had let themselves be disarmed by the 78th Highlanders without a struggle, though unfortunately this did not preclude later

66

retaliatory measures. In Calcutta itself there had indeed been signs of panic, but no looting. Even so, the well-to-do fled their Christian neighborhoods and palaces along the Chowringhee, abandoning their homes and suites to seek protection for themselves and their silverware under the cannons of Fort William.

But as regards the Prussian press attaché, within little more than a year he was back in Berlin—poor once more and cramped under a humble mansard, but rich in Scottish anecdotes, and a free-lance writer.

Now, after the monsoon season, in the cooler nights, the sleepers lie wrapped like mummies. Gray-white sheets mark them stretched out, rolled up on their sides, define back- and belly-sleepers. Often the head is completely covered, the feet exposed, strangely large and well-formed. Callused, cracked soles. Ten feet to a group of five. Beside and before them, baskets, firewood, bundles, cooking pots, brooms, limp bicycle inner tubes.

Quite a few live in half-tents that are propped against house walls, then rolled up at daybreak. Many live, for safety's sake, under the sallow illumination of arc lamps. And everywhere cows are part of the scene.

Here, too, they do their cooking, in the evening, in the morning. During the day a portion of the family stays behind on the spot it has rented through a middleman, and they bang ashes from half-burned coal, chop firewood to sell, rinse bottles, bundle paper.

Their lives pass—often over long years—not as human misery that screams to heaven, but rather as the ultimate possibility for an ordered, day-to-day existence that is unabashedly and solely concerned with an ever-growing family.

The pavement dwellers lie down beside their walls relatively early, around nine o'clock, when the market booths are still open and the aimless throngs still afoot. First the spot for sleeping is swept; it is the brooms that mark the Untouchables.

Accompanied by the writer Gour Kishore Ghosh, off to Calcutta's north side to visit his publisher. A gloomy publishing house with bookstore. After the tour, tea is served. In the warehouse, bundles of books wrapped in old newspapers are piled high. From every printing—two thousand, on the average—only five hundred bound copies are kept in stock. The book dealers pick up the books themselves and earn as much as twenty-five percent on the retail price, the same as the authors. The firm employs twenty people, and its equipment, including the typewriters, keeps faith with the nineteenth century. (Three modern typesetting machines, however, are in operation in rooms adjoining.)

Other writers and a young historian have joined us as well, all in white cotton kept in motion by the fan. The conversation leaps from topic to topic: the peculiarities of the Bengalis, Tagore and his imitators, the partition of the nation (and of the book market), the comparison—out of courtesy, perhaps—with Germany. Finally, even Subhas Chandra Bose. The young historian, with some slight embarrassment, replies to my amazement at the many monuments elbowing Gandhi out of the way: Bose was, after all, a Bengali, even if he did come from Orissa. People see him as a figure of historical dimension. Besides, the aspirations of many Bengalis are bound up with Führer figures. They hope for a new Netaji. And the legend is widespread among the common people: that he is still alive somewhere in the mountains and will return as a hundred-year-old man. On his horse, naturally.

They laugh. And yet it seems to me that they are all (except Ghosh) fixated on Bose.

As a farewell gift, the publisher gives me an illustrated volume titled *Netaji*, a celebration of Bose in photographs: among his family in Cuttack in the state of Orissa; with students in

68

England; after his first arrest; then in exile in Burma; his first time in uniform as commander of the Congress Volunteers; at his desk as mayor of Calcutta and prisoner (frail) in Lucknow; boarding a ship in Bombay; as propagandist and orator for "Free India" in Rome, Milan, Sofia, and Berlin; back again in Calcutta, shaved bald and thinking of his recently deceased father; then in a hospital, surrounded by nephews and nieces; massive at Gandhi's side during the All-India Congress; several times with Nehru; boarding a KLM plane to Europe; in London; in Badgastein, where he went to recover his health; after his landing (healthy once more) at Dum Dum Airport; during the conference in Vishnupur; an enlarged photograph as President of Congress, before microphones, grown stout, in contrast to Gandhi, with Nehru and his skinny daughter Indira; in Santiniketan beside Tagore, hung with garlands; ill on his way to Tripura; healthy again and massive for the announcement of his resignation; then in bitter opposition to Gandhi, as founder of the militant Forward Bloc; as the main speaker at the Anti-Compromise Conference in March of 1940, among adoring crowds in Dacca, where he proclaims the final battle against England; shortly before his capture; then under house arrest; prone, in a hunger strike; then, after his escape, in Berlin, still under the alias of Orlando Marrotta; with the Japanese ambassador Yamamoto, in front of officers of the Indian Legion; beside their instructor, Major Harbich; at the historic handshake with Hitler, among journalists; speaking before companies of the parading Indian Legion; at their swearing the oath of loyalty (to Hitler and to him); then on the conning tower of a German submarine, and beside him, Musenberg, its commander; likewise at sea with his friend Abid Hasan, in a rubber boat that at the end of April takes them to a Japanese submarine; in a group shot with the crew of the Japanese submarine; in Sumatra, May; in Tokyo, June; shortly thereafter as Führer of the Azad Hind Movement; again before microphones as commander-in-chief of the Indian National Army

69

and in uniform among Japanese generals reviewing troops; then a group shot, with his cabinet, among them a woman in uniform; a previous shot of him proclaiming a provisional government; then in boots and leather gloves, Premier Tojo at his side, before a regiment of women; laughing and baring his teeth at some athletic contest; proclaiming total mobilization of all Indians in East Asia, comparable in this to Mussolini; back in Tokyo, with cigarette, in the Japanese sitting position; among Japanese, drinking wine; in Shanghai; Nanking; at last, as Führer-Duce-Netaji, on the Andaman coast gazing (in profile) toward India; in Rangoon, received by the Burmese president, calling for freedom or death; near the front with the INA; again, before microphones shouting To Delhi! To Delhi!; before Imphal, on Indian soil; with vanguard troops in the jungle; beside a telescope, studying the maps of his general staff; back in Tokyo, before cadets; in Bangkok, on the return home, wearing a helmet; and the last photograph, before he climbs aboard his plane, August, 1945 . . .

Yesterday, next door to the Great Eastern Hotel, I bought three posters: Stalin, Kali, Bose—the local Trinity. Daud did the bargaining. Near the poster stand, unemployed men squatting on a heap of gravel. Their arms hanging or crossed, their heels set firm. Not patience, rather submission to a situation that is considered normal, like the climate. The moment such a group squats under a banyan tree, they look as natural as its aerial roots. Drawing: squatters waiting in front of walls, on piles of garbage, under trees.

The three posters are glossy color prints. Whenever I lay them out in a row, Kali ends up in the middle. Stalin and Bose, the former in olive drab uniform, the latter in khaki uniform, are wearing medals. While Kali sticks out her tongue, she smiles.

Early morning, we are picked up by a jeep and brought to the Garbage Mountains, where a Sunday sports festival is to be

70

held for the garbage children. A banner identifies the organizers: "Calcutta Social Project."

Races, running with hands tied, a spoon in the mouth, a marble rolling in the spoon, jumping rope backward and forward, hopping on one leg, fast and slow bicycling, the broad jump. Children and teenagers, from five to eighteen, compete. Decked out with heavily scented flower garlands, attacked by flies, we sit as honored guests under an awning.

Adjacent to the medical shed that houses the athletic equipment and the prizes, a yard where scraps from the nearby Chinese leather factory are cooked with chemical additives, then sieved, dried, and put into sacks as fertilizer. The sour odor drifts our way, but the smell of the garlands dominates. The workers, Moslems of course, earn up to twelve rupees a day.

Next to the yard, the stinking canal and the overpass to the road that leads to the airport. The garbage children who win in the competitions are brought to us. Mrs. Karlekar, whose considerable size makes her vulnerable to the heat, to the flies, awards the prizes. What particularly amazes the children, other than my pipe, is Ute. The girl who won in the spoon race gives me a piece of gum.

Beyond the work area of the leather-scrap cookers the garbage landscape begins—a new layer of fallout. In it, people and cows, above it, vultures and crows. The Garbage Recycling Company is hard at work, day and night (Sundays included). And everywhere, along the roadside and in the gorges of the garbage dump: paper bags stuffed to bursting, bales of tattered plastic, bundled rags, baskets full of shards—even under the arches of the overpass, next to which the children are running another race with their hands tied.

On the horizon behind the Garbage Mountains, the boxed maze of the city with its high rises, water towers, flat roofs, chimneys releasing black smoke, and the double-rowed pylons of power lines. (Somewhere in one of the garbage canyons,

Kali squats atop Siva's pink belly. His head, the sickle to one side. Her blackness overshadowing the torso—or the smoke from the chimneys has eclipsed the sun.)

After lunch with the Karlekars, who are wholly dedicated to helping the garbage and slum children, we drive to Amitava Ray's home on the city's south side. For several days now, they have been rehearsing a still unfinished Bengali translation of my play *The Plebeians Rehearse the Uprising* on their rooftop terrace. Ray is directing and has taken on the most difficult role, the Boss, who simultaneously has to be Coriolanus.

The terrace is hung with faded pink fabric stretched over a bamboo frame quickly thrown together, which extends the cloth around the stage area. One after the other, seven, eight actors arrive. They complain about the bus connections. Most are members of the Communist Party. My question about the difficulties they might have doing a production of *Plebeians*, considered "counterrevolutionary and anticommunist," is answered with laughter. After all, in the second act, a mason smashes a picture of Stalin. What that one man does in anger, the Party should have done long ago.

Amitava Ray rehearses the third act, the tale of the belly and limbs, and the hanging scene that follows. Because the bearded actor who plays Erwin—he delivers the demagogic fairy tale about the all-embracing, all-protecting state—wants to sing it following Bengali theatrical conventions, I suggest that the instrumental accompaniment be assigned to the duped workers; there could hardly be a better way to show how successfully that old trick of slogan chanting works. (After two decades of abstinence, I find myself interested in theater again. Ray's technique—no cult of the director for him; instead, as a matter of course, he consults with the author, spurs me to join in.)

During the rehearsal, endless tea. Racket from the neighborhood. The reverberating noise of someone banging on iron. Toward evening, the conch horns lament. Swarms of crows

72

plummet into the nearby trees. Radio music from open windows. All of which, plus the constant honking of bicycle rickshas, drown out my play. At home, for years now, every stage has refused it, because it runs counter to both Germanys. On the drive home, the gentle parody of Erwin's voice still chanting in my ear, we see the first pavement dwellers squatting beside the cooking fires. How theatrically the fires' reflection falls on the squatters and the sleepers.

Three hours of tangled streets, until, near the river, we happen upon the backdrop of palatial semi-ruins. The portal weighs down on eight columns clutched in the branching talons of trees. The wings are flanked by slender columns laced with rioting creepers.

Without a word, Daud leads us into the palace. The spacious inner courtyard. Facades, once extravagant, now visibly crumbling. The rooms of one wing, lost in abandoned blackness. Rubble, trash, garbage tumble from doors and stairwells. Children playing, pigeons, laundry on poles along the far wall.

Finally a gentleman in the customary pajamas calls down to us from a balustrade of the wing on our right. He is a judge on the High Court and, as the descendant of the former owner, a Mullick, is now the owner (along with six other relatives) of these semi-ruins. He lives in several rooms—absurdly high ceilings—the mezzanine. And now here we sit, invited guests. He tells about himself, about the palace, which dates from the days of Warren Hastings and is one of the oldest palaces in Calcutta, over two hundred years old. Thirty years ago, a fire destroyed the left wing and with it the library. Unfortunately the family is out of funds, and the city cannot maintain this palace any more than it can the others.

Tea is served by a girl who, we are told, is eleven, brought at age eight to the city by her sister. Later the child (without the High Court judge) leads us up a ramshackle winding staircase and onto the rooftop terrace. Daud translates: The girl earns forty rupees (three dollars) a month, and free board. She says she cannot read or write, though the judge's children, somewhat older than she, can. A case of common (and of course illegal) exploitation, but perfectly natural in the judge's eyes. It does not occur to him or his wife, whom we see only in passing, to let the girl be taught along with their own children.

From the roof, a panoramic view across the labyrinth of houses and huts, through the thicket of TV antennas and laundry, as far as Howrah Bridge, which vaults above the river between two great pylons and is considered the city's emblem. Now, toward evening, smoke rises toxic out of chimneys, courtyards, and windows. The pavilion on the terrace is crowned by a mutilated angel. I draw, while behind me Ute and Daud listen to the girl's list of childish wishes. With the last light fading, the girl asks for a photograph of herself, just one, of herself only—like the many photographs the judge's children have.

The river only surmised. As I draw—how delicate the filigree of the bridge as it spans the city lost in shadow upon shadow— I leave space for Kali in the foreground that borders the terrace. Here, she might squat with her sickle. At her feet, coconuts split open. Deftly, because it suits the scene—and crows are on the rise everywhere—she shows her tongue.

Subhas Chandra Bose's initial hope—with the help of the German army, to liberate the subcontinent by invading India across the Caucasus (as Aryan cowherds once did)—was buried at Stalingrad. His second hope—mocking all distance, he planned to ride piggyback on the Japanese army from Burma to the Arabian Sea, while the Indian masses rose up all around him— collapsed before Imphal and was likewise buried in the retreat through Burmese jungles, with heavy losses and the disintegration of the Indian National Army. After Germany surrendered unconditionally in May, 1945, and when Japanese

74

capitulation, following Hiroshima, seemed imminent, Subhas Chandra Bose once again took hope, wide-ranging hope. On the last Japanese plane out, he flew from Singapore in the direction of Manchuria, intending to offer himself as an ally to the invading Russians—all for the good of India. With the help of the Soviet army he would achieve, finally, what had proved impossible with the Germans and then the Japanese: victory over hated British rule. Ever a rash man of bold presumptions, he saw the future: a free India at the side of the powerful Soviet Union.

Landing first in Bangkok and Indochina, the Japanese plane crashed on takeoff at Formosa, its final stopover. Bose died of his injuries. His last words, so it is said, were a promise that India would soon be free. A correct prognosis, but independence (two years later) did not bring the freedom the Netaji had in mind.

And so he lives on, a saint. A documentary of his quixotic life recently shown nationwide on Indian television, including photographs of a wine-tippling Bose surrounded, glass in hand, by Japanese generals, resulted in fierce audience protest (not because of the Japanese, but because of the wine), a protest that might have led to nationwide unrest, had the producers not followed the program with some lulling light entertainment.

Daud has a good nose. Underway with him, this time on Calcutta's south side. Actually, he should be depressed, since he's heard that his residence permit will definitely not be extended. Worse: he is threatened with deportation to Bangladesh. He reports this casually, and hopes—or is childishly confident—that I can help. After all, I've written letters on his behalf.

This time, one of the usual palatial ruins on South End Park. Behind the iron gate, palm trees in a high, even row before the facade, which is blotched, stripped of its stucco. The grand stairway sweeping down out of a riot of vegetation. Columns, balconies, terraces, turrets, dilapidated roofs, rubbled walls, all in the style of Indo-Victorian fussiness. But laundry between columns, on the terraces—the palace is occupied.

Daud says his "Moment please," and already has located the gate in the fence, leads us up the grand staircase, then up unrailed stairs. Plants rioting in the main hall as well, the marble steps loose, open beams where the roof once was, pigeons flying in and out.

On the top floor we are soon encircled. Forty-five families, well over three hundred people, have nidified here, populating the ruin from stables to turrets. As in all slums, here too it is a woman who answers questions. She introduces herself as the community boss. Her husband was murdered by Pakistani soldiers in 1971. Like many Hindu families, she fled with her two children. (A daughter arrives, with schoolbag.)

Now the woman speaks—no, delivers a speech, one she's probably given often. Several times now, a ranking police officer—a Moslem, as you might expect—has come to demand they vacate the premises. She told him that she and all the others were political refugees and that she would kill him, as her husband was killed, if he came again, unless he came to offer housing elsewhere, adequate housing, and that meant water and electricity.

Daud translates. Although he is a Moslem, these people are his countrymen from Bangladesh. (Later I tell him: Daud, write about it.) The palace has its history, of course. It belonged to Ram Singh Bedi—that is, a Sikh—a merchant who died after the First World War. Then a certain Mr. Khetri took possession. Following his death, the palace was vacant for a long time, fell into disrepair, and was known in the neighborhood as the Haunted Castle. Only in 1971, when millions of refugees inundated the city, did Hindu families occupy the still inhabitable shell.

The palace is not just a crumbling stage set. Here families live with their past. Illegally, with no electricity, but with

76

running water. Craftsmen in the stables. In one of the tower rooms, someone (a poet?) is harrying his old-fashioned typewriter. Wherever there's space left along the curlicue-trimmed walls, rows of cow-dung cakes autographed by women and children. On the balustrades, limestone angels, still sound, though with amputations. The driveway to the palace speaks of guests past: colonial officers, newly rich merchants and industrialists, landowners, all pulling up in coaches.

. . . and suddenly, during our preparations for a trip to Madras, Hyderabad, Poona, and, still hoping for a visa, to Burma (ultimately denied us—"Writers Not Wanted!"), suddenly, after Daud has dragged me along to the Barabazar quarter and I am (suddenly) seized by the desire to dive in, to be stirred in with the bubbling human brew that thickens toward noon as it cooks, to lose myself in it, suddenly the taste of return comes strongly: the world awaiting us at home.

The way they greet each other in frozen cheerfulness or with stylized warmth. Shameless, those displays behind burglar-proof glass. What they offer as toys: jokes about the Titanic, Doomsday board games. Their ailments, the ailments of quintessential private patients. Their main concerns: television at breakfast, the half-life of their vegetables. That number after the decimal, the constant increase of the unemployed, becomes more and more boring. Clearance sales. For twelve months on end, Berlin (West and East) is determined to claim that it is seven hundred and fifty years old, just as Calcutta (shortly) will celebrate its three hundred years in slums and palaces. The latest outrage is that the corruption common in the countries of the Third World now finds imitators in the industrial nations. They're supposed to learn from us, not we from them! All school curricula, profit-oriented. One of the required courses is called How to Cope with Grief. And what else? AIDS and the right to self-fulfillment. Relationships in easily transported boxes. The dollar's dropsy. Flick scandal? Old hat. In its stead,

77

matters of taste reduced to headlines. And now even the telephone booths are gussied up postmodern. Stylized shit lies in toilet bowls. Nowadays, you are with it, you have what you have, you stay cool. (And every shampoo and set is worth an Indian's week's wages.)

Where were you? In Calcutta. Ghastly place, isn't it?

Temporary good-bye to the Garbage Mountains, to the rice, fish, dhal, and oversweet coconut cakes, to the Calcutta Social Project, to Amitava Ray's actors, to Shuva, who is still worried about his "arts acre," and to Daud, who is afraid of the police and plans to take to the back-country by year's end.

By way of Madras and Hyderabad we intend to fly to Poona, visit friends just before the New Year. The books (Fontane, too) stay behind in Lake Town, as do the ironing board and my drawings.

Long horns of cows painted in bright colors sweep past the hump on their backs, bronze bells fastened to their tips tinkling. The white cotton here whiter than elsewhere, against the darker skin. Southern India, land of the Dravidians. Madras, even more than Calcutta, brainchild of the British, rocked at present by strife with Tamils and by other crises—the people do not want to speak Hindi, the language decreed by Delhi.

From the beginning, cows were a motif. In the National Museum, bronzes from the Chola period, reminiscent in their grace of Greek terra-cottas. Also the pilot-project temples in Memalapuram (each one hewn from a single stone and serving as pattern for all later temples), and, even more clearly, the two extensive bas-reliefs, long as legends—all distinguished by cows. During the first half of the seventh century, the Pallava dynasty was responsible for the development of the style. Fields of stones full of huge erratics and the ample cliffs may have invited them to experiment and set up workshops.

On the drive back to Madras, we visit a fishing village where monks from Kerala maintain a school. Here, the fishermen

78

own their boats and nets. Christians and Hindus live side by side. (Not a Brahman in the village.) You would like to trust such peace.

The hotel lobby, hung with Christmas knickknacks. We've barely arrived in Madras, and I miss Calcutta. The good food (and wine) in the hotel restaurant, a small luxury that Ute finds pleasant. (For me, it's a cheap silk shirt.)

Temples bursting with color and, quite correctly, off-limits to unbelievers. Colonial palaces, their facades a bawdy union of local and imported architectural styles. The open harbor, dredged from the sea. All slums ousted from the cityscape.

At our visit to a dance and music school—which, and not so long ago, attempted reforms based on those established by Tagore in Santiniketan—we come upon Indian melancholy: out of the crumbling, chaotic rubble between the dance and music studios, drift the sounds of the sitar, accompanied by tabla and the slapping of bare feet. Time fleeting according to schedule.

Christmas, what is Christmas? We are in Hyderabad, a Moslem enclave. Whether from the ruins of the caravansaries or the heaped collection of domed graves of Moslem rulers, whether from flawless arches or severe facades: everything, every geometric mosaic, every window grated with filigree, speaks against Christmas. Even the green parrots, nesting in the domed graves, mock the Glad Tidings.

We live outside the city, amid hills stamped with erosion. Gigantic crags, washed bare, rise up out of stony fields. Boulders, piled in towers, wedged together, cloven. Construction materials for an upper class that plants its ostentatious villas in deserts of stone. Between construction sites and next to quarries cower the slum huts of the construction workers, who are migrants. The hardness of the material strengthens, petrifies the polarities of rich and poor, up and down. Show your tongue! If only Kali would come, and go to work.

A hundred years ago, the region was wooded, we are told,

79

and a favorite hunting ground for nizams addicted to pomp. Later, in photographs, we see rows of Anglo-Indian hunting parties behind their booty: tigers lying likewise in rows. A wall, studded with broken glass, surrounds a good-sized estate that belongs to the last Nizam of Hyderabad, now living in Australia. The scrap of overgrown jungle in the center of a stony desert hints at the landscape of the past. Since the owners of the posh villas have had deep wells bored everywhere, the groundwater level is sinking; only the devastation is growing.

Christmas morning, we climb the still-undeveloped slopes. I draw, Ute reads, leaning against a boulder. Silence. Only the regular tapping of invisible stonemasons, a sound that reminds me of my apprentice years: limestone, Silesian marble, tufa, basalt . . .

We walk through the old city; on one side, the four towers of the Charminar. Smells, long-legged goats, the horns of the water buffalo painted red, Moslem women draped in black, their glances following us across the rim of the cloth. Curiosity, which, because all the rest is veiled, comes as a particularly naked revelation.

In the country we visit a weaving village, ostensibly a co-operative. But it turns out that here, too, five villages (six hundred looms) are ruled by one family. The material is delivered to the weavers, and they are paid by the piecework. All around, barren land. Mountains like mounds of stone someone just dumped there. Then a long stretch of palm trees, from which palm wine is drawn. Hanging clay bottles fill with rising sap. Beside the road, a vendor's stand. The wine has a raw, fermented odor but a mild taste.

On the drive back, by the highway, five miles long and six years old, a German-Indian development project, which consists of potholes and nothing more. We spot, off to one side, a wagon-mountain, oxcarts loaded with hay. We stop. Nomads, wrapped in black and dark-brown blankets for the night, squat in groups around fires within the closed ranks of their

80

carts, oxen lying about them. They rise up to greet us; they have come from another century.

The next day, the Nizam Palace, full of precious vulgarities. Up the stairs, the ascending gallery of ancestors from the days of colonial rule: portraits of British governors-general and viceroys, from Warren Hastings down to Lord Wavell. Bohemian chandeliers. The dining table for eighty people, the nizam's chair on a low dais. From a high terrace we gaze out over the southern edge of the old town, across the city, to the surrounding countryside, stony desolation. In the haze, like outlined shadows, domed graves of princes, the lofty fortress of Golconda. And behind the terrace, too, which adjoins the "women's wing," we see stony desert, though nearer the city it is littered with settlements.

In Hyderabad there are four hundred thirty slums, in which about a million people live, not counting nameless unregistered slums. Although these slums are less extensive and have wider lanes (above the sewers) than the slums of Calcutta, their tales of misery are much the same. In three rooms, twenty-five people. Few children go to school. Hindus and Moslems, we are assured, live in peaceful neighborliness as long as the politicians don't set them at each other's throats. In one slum, a one-room school, where eighty children are taught in two shifts; the children attend irregularly because they can earn a day's wages working. The teacher, a state employee, earns three hundred seventy rupees a month. A school meal is provided each morning.

Our flight leaves Hyderabad on time. In Bombay, after a two-hour wait, we learn that the plane to Poona has been canceled. By taxi, past a seemingly endless slum, said to be Asia's largest, into the city, to the counter for overland cars. There are five of us, plus driver, for the eighty-mile trip that takes over four hours. Ute and I sit in front; despite the aggressive driving, we are glad that we didn't fly.

The road is flat at first, then climbs, finally crosses a pass in multiple curves, then moves through dry country. No trees: rock formations, wide and barren. Each town we pass, each factory, all the quarries and larger road-construction sites are bordered by small to medium-sized slums. In some places the center of town is a slum. And beside all the new developments—two-storied, flat-roofed concrete boxes—stretch, as if they were part of the plan, double and triple rows of slums.

All the way to Poona, the road is flanked by banyan trees, their trunks bandaged at the driver's eye level by stripes of white-red-white. Poona, too, is saturated with slums; 35 to 40 percent of its 1.3 million inhabitants live in slums. Poona is expensive, perhaps because the colony of European souls, who have put their brains in storage with the local guru (recently returned), is driving up prices. Besides, the climate is tolerable.

With the help of a motorized ricksha, we find Adi Patel's house. He lives in what was once the English officers' mess, in the center of a military base now occupied by the families of high-ranking Indian officers. (The transfer of keys from army to army had gone without a hitch.)

A central room big as a barn, with small rooms on the sides. Several dogs, an eight-year-old boy, a fifteen-year-old spastic daughter, the old servant, and Adi's wife, who is named Dagmar and comes from the German Sauerland. He is a Parsi, a two-hundred-pounder, who rows with his arms when he walks and (always cheerful) is in charge of all the Indian projects of the relief organization Terre des hommes. Here, amid the usual resolutions, we are to start the new year. Lesson one: Show your tongue . . .

Then on the road for two days in the Patels' Ford: Adi, Dagmar, the son, Ute, and I. It was, by Adi's calculation, a one-hundred-seventy-mile drive south to the border of Karnataka. We drive through Maharashtra on the best highway (so far) in India, and, as on the way from Bombay to Poona, under banyan trees. Just outside Poona, we cross one pass of

82

medium altitude, then a steeper one. Fields of millet, then sugarcane spread out around us. Halfway there, more passes, then a flat plateau. The mountains are all treeless, cut by gorges, their layered profiles readable.

As we drive along, I draw what comes our way: oxcarts viewed from the front. Until well into the evening, the footpaths on either side of the road are crowded in both directions. Women, men, children too, burdens on their heads. Beside gravel pits, quarries, and sugarcane mills crouch the slumlike settlements of nomads and seasonal workers. No view without people in it.

Here, as flayed and emaciated as the land is, India seems strong, and even the villages are held together by a will to survive. But in the larger towns we drive through, everything, no sooner than it is built, starts to crumble; all the planning, only half carried out, leads to chaos.

Cross-country for almost a hundred and eighty miles: no woods, no reforestation, and yet everywhere searchers for wood, children and old women. A load of a few sticks after a daylong search. Computers tabulate, project the course of this soundless process, this urgent, barefoot, accelerating destruction; they know how many (or how few) years it will take to turn vast regions of India into desert.

Everywhere, we get glimpses of remote centuries. In a sugarcane mill, mountains of cane straw to heat the two fires burning around the clock under shallow pans. Estimated diameter of the pans: twelve feet. From each pan, lifted first on bamboo rods as thick as your arm, then gently tipped to drain, the cooks fill six thirteen-gallon tubs of syrup. Beautiful honey-yellow cakes are piled upside-down like cones of wax. But the first draw from each pan is a plate-sized disk offered to the gods. Eight of these consecrated disks lie in a wooden trough: the day's ration so far.

Close to the cooking spot and beside an equally antiquated steam-driven cane cutter, are low huts for the families of the seasonal workers, made of cane stalk, roofed with cane leaves.

Just beyond Kolhapur (still in the state of Maharashtra) the sugarcane fields come to an end; until we reach Nipani (in Karnataka now) the crop is chiefly tobacco. In one of the many tortuously meandering small towns, several tobacco factories are in operation. Here the harvest, crudely cut, just as it comes from the fields via wholesalers, is shredded in several stages until the tobacco is ready to be rolled into Beedi cigarettes. The collected dust is turned into snuff.

Adi Patel wants to introduce us to a project supported by Terre des hommes. A teacher and a doctor have organized the tobacco workers, all women. Four thousand of them work in Karnataka, and an estimated forty thousand in the state of Gujarat.

No sooner do we arrive than we visit a factory—and find it hard to believe that this is not an exception we see but the typical conditions of employment. Through the office, with its fancy colonial furniture, into the factory courtyard. In the elongated rectangle before us, an immobile yellow dust cloud envelops a dozen women who turn the tobacco, sift it, turn it again, in endless repetition. Inside the factory hall, two light bulbs are barely discernible. Here thirty women work amid shredding machines, jittery sifting boxes, and ventilators not intended for renewing the air but for separating the tobacco from its dust as it is shaken out of flat baskets.

The intense, sweet odor of Beedis. The women's bright saris, their arms, hands, feet, and faces powdered a yellowish brown. We fight for air. The women break into condescending but friendly laughter at Ute's coughing fit. The forewoman assures us that one quickly gets used to it. Beginners are advised to chew tobacco while they work. And this, for nine hours a day. A few years ago, before there was a union, fourteen- to sixteen-hour workdays were the rule. Eyebrows, eyelashes as though dusted with brown flour. The women's faces seem burned out by the work. Only if Adi or Dhruv, the doctor, speaks to

84

them, do they respond with laughter. Slowly, through the dust, we make out bracelets on arms, rings on toes.

Later, a meeting of workers from other factories at the house of a teacher. Union issues are the topic. Several workers have not yet paid their dues, or do so irregularly. About sixty women, still dusty, hunker back on their heels, weary but concentrating all the same.

The Beedi odor hangs over the assembled semicircle. Several women, whom we thought to be in their seventies, are only in their early fifties. They have been on the factory payroll for more than thirty years. The monotone report of two union officials. We have been thrust back a hundred years, more, though one official pulls documents out of a briefcase much like the attaché cases used in international commerce.

The union distributes cards on which the working days are recorded; by attesting seniority, they provide protection against layoffs. In the center of the semicircle squats the spokeswoman, a robust matron whose questions and answers are accented with gestures. At the moment, there are no complaints at the plant. The workers agree to their daily wage of eleven rupees, even though they're entitled to twenty-four. That's the wage scale in the state of Kerala. The issue at present is how to get the women year-round job security, since there is sufficient raw material in stock to last the twelve months of the year.

The plant owners insist on seasonal employment. This allows them to lay off the old crew and hire younger women not yet worn out by the work. The union cards show a yearly average of two hundred sixty working days, a number inconsistent with seasonal production. But since the owners have the upper hand in the local courts, the union intends to appeal to the Supreme Court in New Delhi.

I am asked to speak to the women. I tell them about the beginnings of the union movement in Europe, about the printers and cigar-wrappers in Hamburg-Altona. Once upon a time . . .

85

After our meal, we gather in the assembly hall to watch slides whose theme is the adoration of a goddess to whom all temple prostitutes are consecrated. Many of the tobacco workers were prostitutes at one time and have been won over to tobacco production through the efforts of the union. A questionable improvement, since many are still bound to their pimps, the temple Brahmans, because as women "consecrated to the goddess" they enjoy higher social status. In the rigid hierarchical system, tobacco workers rank lower even than the women who wrap the Beedis. Not until they were organized by the union did these women gain enough self-respect to be able to confront the plant owner. Formerly, one of the women tells us, they would cover their faces in his presence, but nowadays . . . With a disparaging gesture she hints at the potential of the future.

The next morning, we visit a cooperative, where the workers can buy their state-subsidized rations of rice, wheat, lentils, kerosene, etc., at a reasonable price and obtain credit (without the normal usury). In what was once a stable, windowless, the workers' small children are watched over by two older women. Like a herd in its pen, the children squat, cheek to cheek, on bast mats.

In the administration building of another tobacco plant, young men lounge in wicker chairs and gape at a TV screen: the management. A few steps across the courtyard, then through a double door, and we are standing in a cloud of dust. Scrawny old men dragging heavy sacks. About eighty women are employed here on a seasonal basis. In the yellow-brown fog we recognize participants from the union meeting and are greeted by laughter. Constant references to a workday that no longer lasts fourteen hours, as had been the case only a few years before. A mere nine, now. Adi Patel's gurgling, rolling German: Progress, no?

Back to the TV-addicted management in the administration building. Nowhere, not even at great construction sites, where

86

women carry tremendous loads on their heads, have I seen more clearly the dichotomy between an emaciated lower class and a lazy middle class. And once again I summon causes, effects, and bid Indian, Brazilian slums, the slums of the world, to put down their roots right beside the Deutsche Bank.

Before our drive back, we were shown, in the union hall, slides on the growing and processing of tobacco. But photographs tell you nothing. The room is filled with the dusty odor of yesterday's working women. . . .

Back through the karst. What is India? An occasion for publishing handsome picture books in color or black and white? The legacy of the British Empire: a great power on crutches? Or the last hope of bankrupt reason? What is there here to be revitalized?

All the statistics, even the doctored ones, add up to unanimous columns of impoverishment, exodus from the land, cities turned to slums. Who slaughters whom and where is recorded daily by a thousand and more newspapers—the wealth of languages. And further consequences: the dwindling of forest equals the growth of desert. And birthrates, approximations after the decimal point. Every year India grows by about seventeen million people—the equivalent of the population of the German Democratic Republic, even after subtracting those who leave it. By the year 2000, which the world has decided is cause for celebration, eight hundred million Indians will have grown to one billion. Words like chaos and catastrophe are common usage among commentators; but the question of whether a revolution could provide redress will not be answered by Marx or Mao. It will be answered by Kali with her sickle.

On the road approaching us: above the central slum of a town (just before Poona), a large billboard hawks the Rotary Club.

Male Indians on foot between villages—the way they cross

87

their arms behind their backs by grabbing the left elbow in the right hand.

Unfailingly cheerful, Adi Patel answers my questions with dreary facts. A mountain of flesh always on the move, refusing to be discouraged. Later—on our way to the Bombay airport now—he shows us a ramshackle settlement where "tribals" are quartered, India's remaining aborigines (there are fifty million of them), who have been driven out of the neighboring villages. On fields they once owned, they now work for starvation wages. Serfs, who under the pressure of the caste system (and its radical right-wing Hindu party called the Shiv Sana) have had to sell their land for a pittance. Nowhere do they have legal protection, because both the police and the judges have been corrupted, and for the few politically committed attorneys in Bombay this region (fifty miles away) is too remote.

We look forward to Calcutta. . . .

Laundry stretched between bamboo poles. Rising above the flat roofs, stored atop slum huts, bamboo—stockpiled for tents, high rises, grandstands, scaffolding. (In Baruipur the bamboo grove is taller than the spreading mangrove tree.) Bamboo for every purpose.

Home from our trip, here I am, as promised, at the dedication of "arts acre." Shuva looks happy. His face: constant amazement, framed by hair on chin and head. No mention of the intrigues, the hurts, the imprisonment. He leads us, the first group of visitors, through the exhibition pavilion, where my etchings are hung. On a bronze plaque embedded in the wall next to the date of dedication, my name is engraved. In the first finished studio, tea is served in paper cups. In the evening, Bengali poets read their poetry.

While the reading goes on, I make notes on my sketchpad: daily fare—rice, dhal, and a mouthful of low-cal poems . . . From the nearby villages, figures wrapped in cloths and blankets keep to the periphery, aliens. Nineteen different poets read

88

for us. It sounds like rain: Tagore, Tagore. So many watered-down realities. The last plane to Dacca takes off from Dum Dum Airport.

During the day, the rehearsals continue. I try to attenuate the actors' penchant for melodramatic gestures by my own acting, by demonstrating that humor is also a part of the plebeians' tragedy. Because of their limited mimetic vocabulary (in comparison to European actors), every movement is exaggerated: agitated gaits, menacing gestures. We are rehearsing in a spacious tin shed that was all the rage in the sixties and early seventies, in the days of Bengali polit-theater (and of the Naxalite uprisings). Sundry cats romp on the tin roof, which bothers me more than it does the actors.

In the meantime, I have been hot on the heels of the immigration police, trying to recover our papers missing since Dacca; we're told they'll be in our hands by tomorrow.

Moments in passage: empty barrels of tar. The street devours tar without ever getting its fill, half its fill.

Huts in front of palaces, slums at the door. The slum is well on its way to occupying the palace. It will be a clean, hard sweep. Where is the middle class?

Assembled near the hammer and sickle, they crouch under their symbol as it slips on the crumbling wall.

He gives a friendly, uncomprehending smile when I suggest that, now that "arts acre" has been successfully dedicated (and before new aggravations set in), he give up the chairmanship. After joining Shuva for dinner (rice, dhal, fish) on College Row—this neighborhood stays lively well into the night—we buy an extra suitcase.

Images, everywhere. They must not be allowed to cancel one another. How that kid there with the headband, barely out of the house, empties garbage, then several buckets of ashes into the street. His eyebrows are grown together. In the distance, a crow flying toward us. Or the old Sikh taxi driver

89

who is a learned scribe. Or the man with the endless shawl wrapped around his head, his shoulders, his body.

Stay here. A portrait of the cracking pavement. Move in very close on the hovels, note the materials. How the strangeness becomes familiar—and remains strange. Forget the twaddle about art. Do decay with a broad brush, with the edge of the pen, with crumbling charcoal. Our mad black mother, how she gives and takes. A cohort of squatters, a cohort of crows. Coconuts, decapitated, split open, piled high. Begin all over again. Re-sort the garbage. Put the bamboo scaffolding up around the high rises. The piles of sticks and logs. The burdens on their heads, casually carried, as though suspended in midair. Count the drying dung cakes on the walls. Or follow a single cow for a day: how she grazes on garbage, is an island in traffic, how she lies in the shadows, is fleetingly a resting place for crows, how—late now—she watches over the sleep of pavement dwellers. . . . But the suitcases are all packed.

Yesterday we experienced our sixth full moon over Bengal. Ute wanted to hold out for that long; and she held out. She came along, was right there, even during the last days, in the dust of the dry season, her eyes tearing. (Where could we have been closer to each other than in commuter trains, in afternoon traffic jams, among the laboring fumes of funeral pyres, or exhausted under our mosquito net?)

This morning, off to see the consul general. The conversation with the affably rumbling consul. Daud's chances are not unpromising. I should write a letter to Foreign Minister Genscher. Only he can help in Daud's case. . . . (But, Daud, how will you be able to live in our cold? The ambience, I mean, not just the climate! What will taste good to you, after fish, dhal, and rice? And your language, will it follow you?)

Then, on our own behalf, to the immigration police, Andul Road. The bureaucratic tone of East Berlin: our papers are not

90

back. No departure without papers. Only the fans moving. Under the surge of air, bright glass balls hold down the stacks of flutter-crazed files. (Daud doesn't want to translate for us all the soft advice he gives—in Bengali, with an urgent smile —to the bureaucrat in charge. Inquire again, day after to-morrow.

The lessons of experience lie deep in Daud's bones, and he suggests we search the floor above us. There we find our papers, as if by accident. The bureaucratic tone softens.

. . . and between rehearsals and final visits we drive through the north side of Calcutta to Kar Medical College, a hospital in the midst of sprawling slums. The facade of the main build-ing was given a coat of ocher paint a few days ago, because a visit by the Prime Minister had been announced. With a union official as his guide, however, Radjiv Gandhi took a different route, which led to forceful expression of outrage suitable for quotation—the election had already begun—so that his outrage was in all the papers the next day.

This same union official, whom Daud quickly locates, leads us through the women's clinic. Too swiftly past mothers and newborns, in beds placed one up against the other, between rows of beds, on floors where trash lies about, past too few nurses. On through grimy rooms where medical equipment rots in disuse. Finally to the emergency room, where, following regulations, we have to remove our shoes and stand barefoot in the filth. Swiftly past piles of blood-drenched bandages, into a blackened kitchen that cooks, it seems, for the netherworld. Everything, especially the underbelly, is to be shown to us: through rear courtyards—garbage everywhere, stopped drains, open sewage—into the courtyard of the university clinic, the largest in the country, we are told.

In front of the lecture building, the Untouchables who work in the morgues are bivouacked in raggedy tents. For several

91

days now, the air-conditioning in the morgue is out of order. The Untouchables are the most zealous blood donors; a kind of part-time job. Equally zealous, a group of self-important young men busy everywhere, managing this source of income for their own profit.

Inside the lecture building, danger of collapse. A large hole in the ceiling, from an accident that occurred some two months before. We marvel at the hole, the debris left behind. The union official points out deficiencies as if they were scenic wonders.

There are 750 students registered at this public hospital, with its 1,087 beds for normally more than 2,000 patients. All of which is known as a permanent state of affairs, whether the Communists or the Congress Party is in power.

Next we visit the English cemetery near Park Street, as an antidote of rest and relaxation, as it were. Under ancient trees, decomposing gravestones. Lots of fat crows—their heads held at an omniscient tilt. Puritan epitaphs; you want to read on forever. Only a few reached ripe old age here. Some graves are well-tended. Fontane again injects his voice. For every Scottish name hewn in stone—in his day, Calcutta was called Scotland's graveyard—he knows legends and bloodcurdling anecdotes. We are happy to listen, though with some impatience.

That evening we attend the first performance of *Plebeians* at the Academy Theater. It's not in the least remarkable that the German journalists, normally so eager to ask about my daily bowel movements, show no interest in a Bengali production of my "German Tragedy." (The *Spiegel*—its dander up, apparently regarding my refusal of an interview as lèse majesté —sicced a spy on us while we were still living in Baruipur. He was only doing his journalist's alternative service, and in time-honored professional style went through and wrote down our private trash.)

92

After the performance, we have dinner with several of the actors at Amitava Ray's home. I am grateful to him because he has lessened the distance I feel to the theater; at moments he even let me set that distance aside. (Maybe write a piece for him and his actors, something that takes place in one of the three thousand slums and deals with Netaji's global adventures. The setting could be the slum that keeps its distance around the circular monument of his bust. In the first act, someone moving from hovel to hovel, taking up a donation for Kali Puja . . .)

Yesterday, the second performance of *Plebeians* in the overcrowded tin shed, on a stage too small. They have speeded up the last two acts. The hairdresser tougher. The ping-pong game with the Party poet almost works; but he needs to be pressed harder as go-between. Ray gives a solid interpretation—from rigid to light-footed—of the Boss (who simultaneously is Coriolanus). The hanging scene is hampered by inadequate stagecraft. Again the cats, performing their own play on the roof.

Today (finally) at Writers' Building, an edifice from British days, where once the young gangsters of the East India Company made fast money, the yuppies of yesteryear. At present, approximately six thousand men and women—who cannot be fired—occupy its several floors, busy only with themselves. In shared offices they sit and shoot the bull. They drink tea, read newspapers, doze. Some of them, moving as though in a trance, shift files around; others sleep, unabashed. Many of the chairs under the fans are empty. A good quarter of the employees moonlight in other offices or are jobbing at the markets. A concentrated assembly of the shiftless middle class. Trash in the corridors, the open stairwells, the inner courtyard. Some of the light-shafts and barricaded exits (they threaten to collapse) are full of garbage. Knee-deep rubbish in corners. In the halls, tea shops and cookshops. And between them, petitioners in the customary squatting position, who may have been waiting for weeks, months, years now. In contrast to the cows: unhorned patience.

We are introduced to the minister of culture. Embarrassed chitchat. Above him on the wall, Tagore and Lenin. We leave quickly (without tea). Just as Prem Chand once wrote his bitter village tales from close up, stories here would have to be filtered through backroom files. . . .

More corridors, more floors. In every office, dusty bundled papers, piles of them, high as wardrobes, never disturbed, unless by the draft of the fans. Here—where nothing is decided, everything postponed, subjected to routine corruption or filed away among other filed-away files—all the threads come together. Here, for years now, just as Congress did, the Left-Front government, the CPI(M) sits in command, continuing to live off advance payments of hope.

The employees' salaries range between eight hundred and two thousand rupees a month; in slum schools comparable to the one run by the Calcutta Social Project, a teacher earns, on average, four hundred rupees. (Daud claims that several dozen "moonlighted" poems emerge daily from these oversized offices. The Writers' Building, once the control room of British colonial dealings and thus well-drilled in sober exploitation, has turned into a hotbed of Bengali lyric poetry.) We leave the parasites' palace, laughing.

Close by, the stock exchange. One atop the other, in wooden boxes painted blue and green, squat the brokers, thick and thin. There are a dozen such stalls; in each of them, the peep show of wild gesticulation. Clad in white cotton, stretched to bursting, or loosely fluttering in the wind—answering several phones simultaneously. They call out bids, flail, accept and convey by finger signal whatever the dense crowd of stock-market customers offers or buys. In the background, the roar of traffic. Nothing can distract these brokers. No other role has been written for them. Daily, they perform a new theatri-

94

cal spectacle, in which (at the moment) the dollar is falling, Swiss francs and German marks are rising, and the rupee plunges lower and lower. The English pound, too, has seen better days. . . .

Then on through alleyways, dim passages in back courtyards seemingly with no exit. And everywhere, teeming life mixed with garbage. Everyone loading or unloading, dragging, shoving their burdens, producing, displaying, offering for sale. But where are the buyers?

Noon, after the third performance of the *Plebeians* at the Academy Theater, we take our leave of all the actors. The familiar drive home courts our final attention: between blocks of houses, a garbage-filled square under siege by searching children. Across the railroad bridge: left, right, the bordering slums, in a Sunday mood today. Laundry above the hovels, public cleaning of teeth, the chatter of people squatting on the conduits that run across the bridge. On the tiniest of unoccupied spaces, coconut fibers spread out to dry. Then from odor to stench, the unforgettable triangle: on the left, the walled-in Chinatown, its leather factories; on the right, the Calcutta Boating Resort, a recreation center with pedal-boats on a pond and with inviting wooden decks lined with bright umbrellas, pennants, Campa Cola ads; and, at the edge of the same pond, twelve fires of a good-sized laundry—over the fires, vats in which rags are boiled, the tatters surrendered by the garbage. Beyond the pond, Dhapa begins: flat at first, where it's been leveled, then freshly dumped mountains of garbage, rounded knolls here, steep cliffs there, notched by canyons; vultures, crows above; and, amid the garbage, people who know no Sunday. In contrast, the small factories on the left, where black smoke does not wallow today. On the right, the sports stadium, its grounds a desolation; new housing developments, slums at their sides. In the foreground, water towers, coconut palms looking small beside the billboards advertising washing machines, console

95

televisions, refrigerators. Then concrete culverts, with residents; a sewage canal wrapped in rampant green; and, just before the pepper factory that announces we're in Lake Town, the final scenes. Two cows lying as if in conversation. From the roofs of their huts, slum children fly kites. On her way to market, Kali with a basket on her head, full of freshly hacked coconuts.

She had never been here, had never wanted to come. He, years ago, had come alone and, horrified by the city, had wanted to get away. And once away, had wanted to return. (For reasons that became a familiar litany to him, he had long been seeking a precise word for shame.) The horrifying city, the terrible goddess within, would not let him go.

They took other trips together. But everywhere, he would say: When I was in Calcutta five years ago, seven years ago, nine years ago . . . He made comparisons and preparations; she didn't. One whole year—he wanted to spend there (she would have to hold out there) one whole year. When they flew off, and the children (old enough by now) were left behind, there were other reasons—hurts, disgust, up-to-here—the reasons he wanted to fly from, leave behind.

Eleven years later, he came back. They took the train, cross-country, from Bombay. They had taken precautions. A steamer trunk, heavy with books, preceded them. Not just he, the city too had changed. High rises and subway construction—what looked like progress. But the decay was progressing, too. You see, he said, on Howrah Bridge, where eleven years ago vendors squatted side by side, left and right. They've cleared them out. The Communists are running things now.

Once they were there, both of them, the city was a horror for her, but no longer for him. He sprang to life; she lived less and less. It's the climate, the misery, the indifference, and because there's nothing I can do, she said. He wrote and sketched,

96

sketched and wrote. His question, offhanded or so it seemed, every now and then: Should we leave?

When they shipped the steamer trunk back and bought an extra, a fourth suitcase, he said: If we ever come back here, we'll take Fontane with us again. . . .

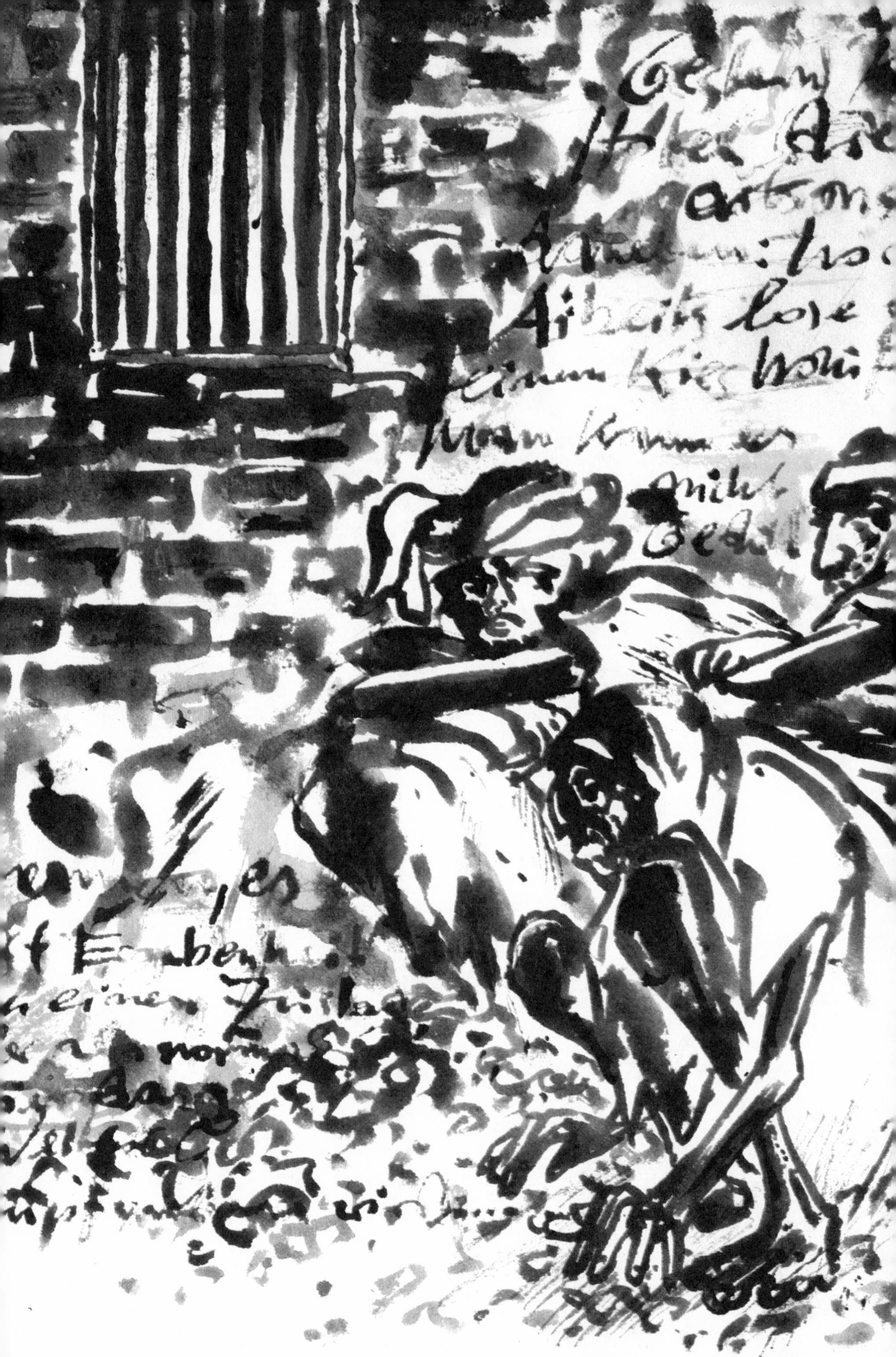
Man kann es
nicht

ich neben dem Great Easter
Stalin, Kali, Bose, die
Dreieinigkeit.

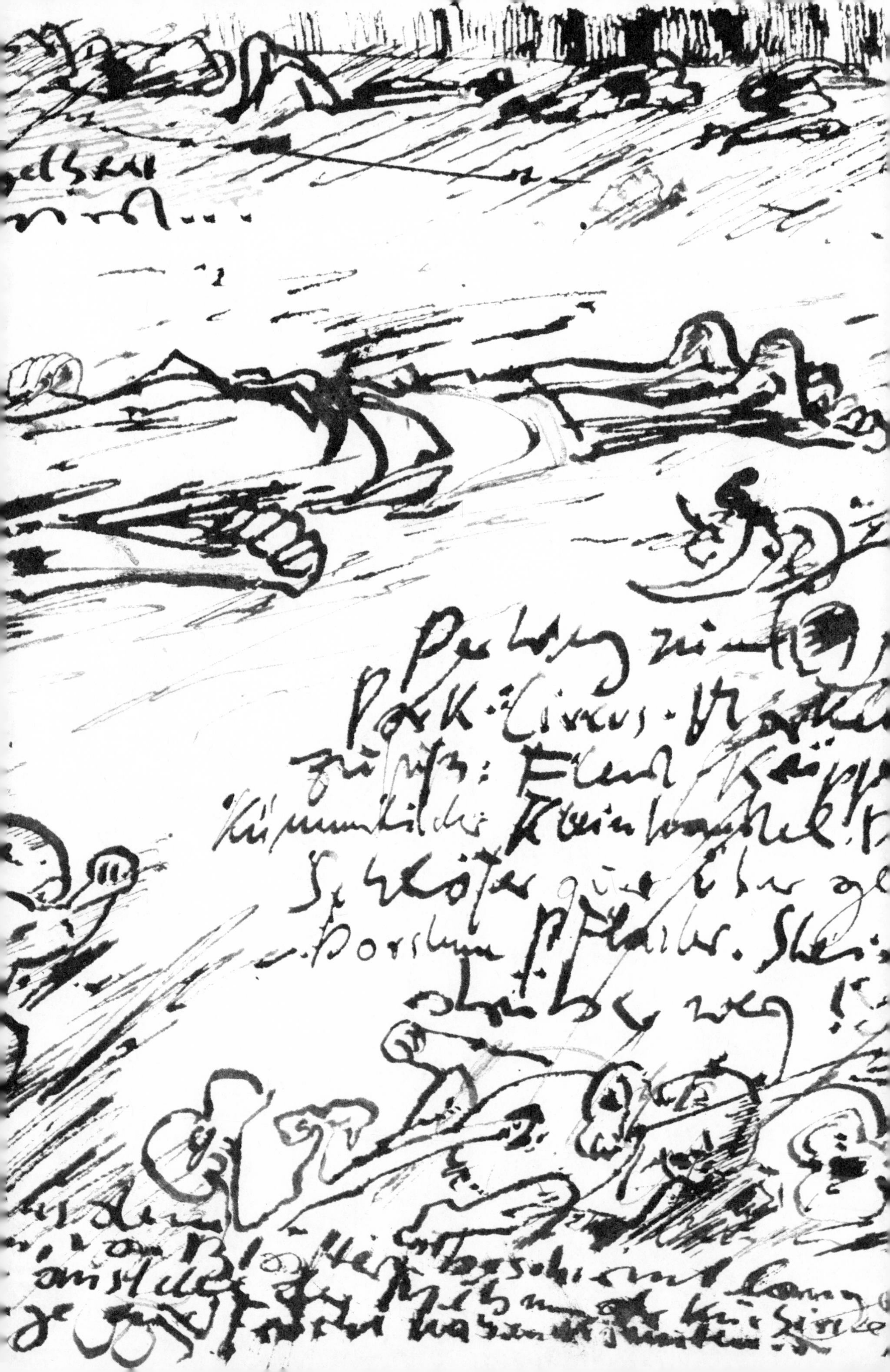
Park · Zirkus ·
Elend

Auf dem Maidan vorm [illegible]
Bischof an der [illegible]
[illegible] links und rechts
Banyanbaum, der an der [illegible]
[illegible] sie [illegible]
[illegible] Sichel
und Hammer ähnlich
den Kontrahenten [illegible]
Kommunisten [illegible]
[illegible]

[illegible] den Bade- und
[illegible] von vier grünen
Gesicht, die den [illegible]
[illegible]
[illegible] deren Augen
wie [illegible]

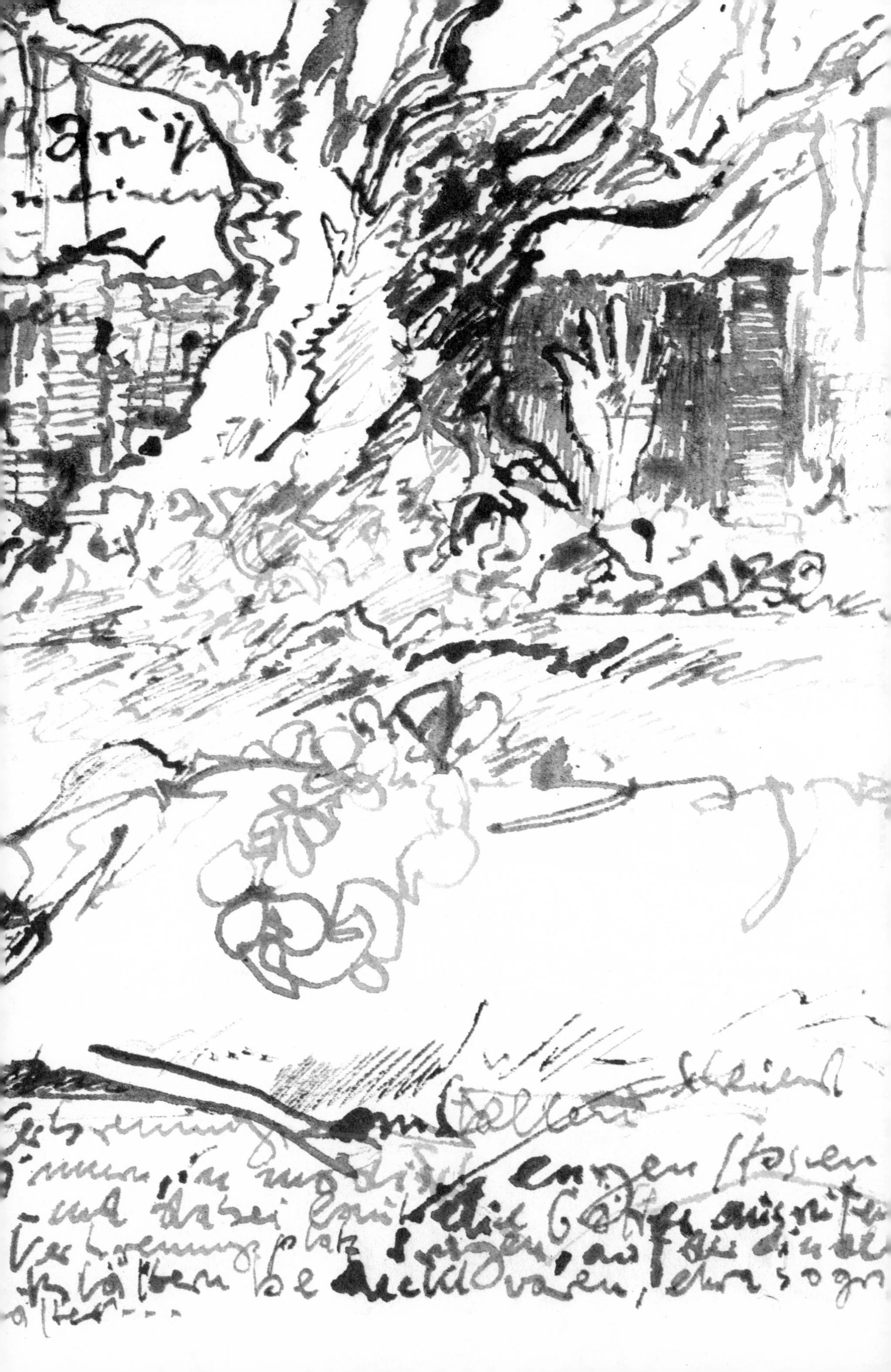

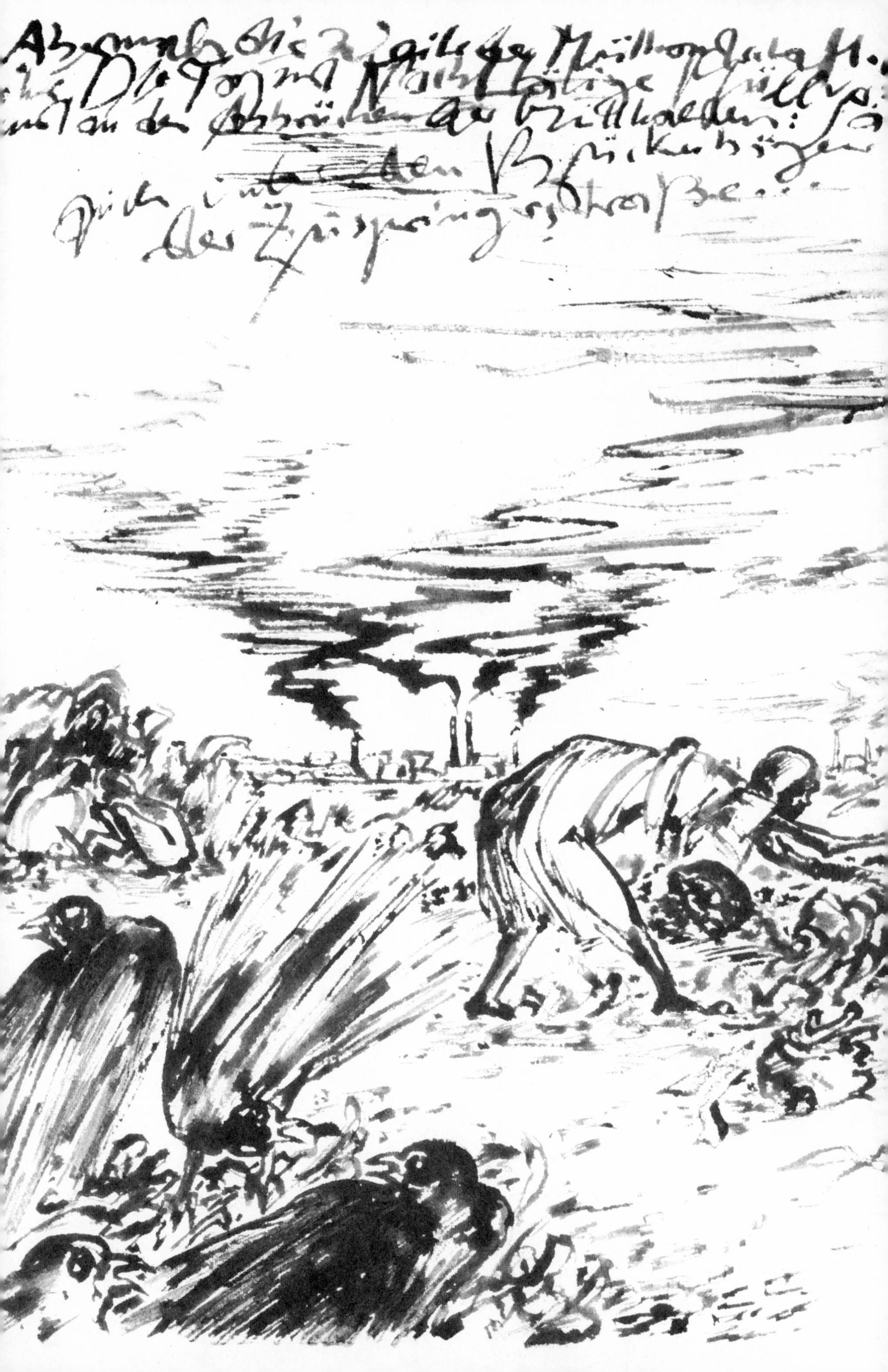

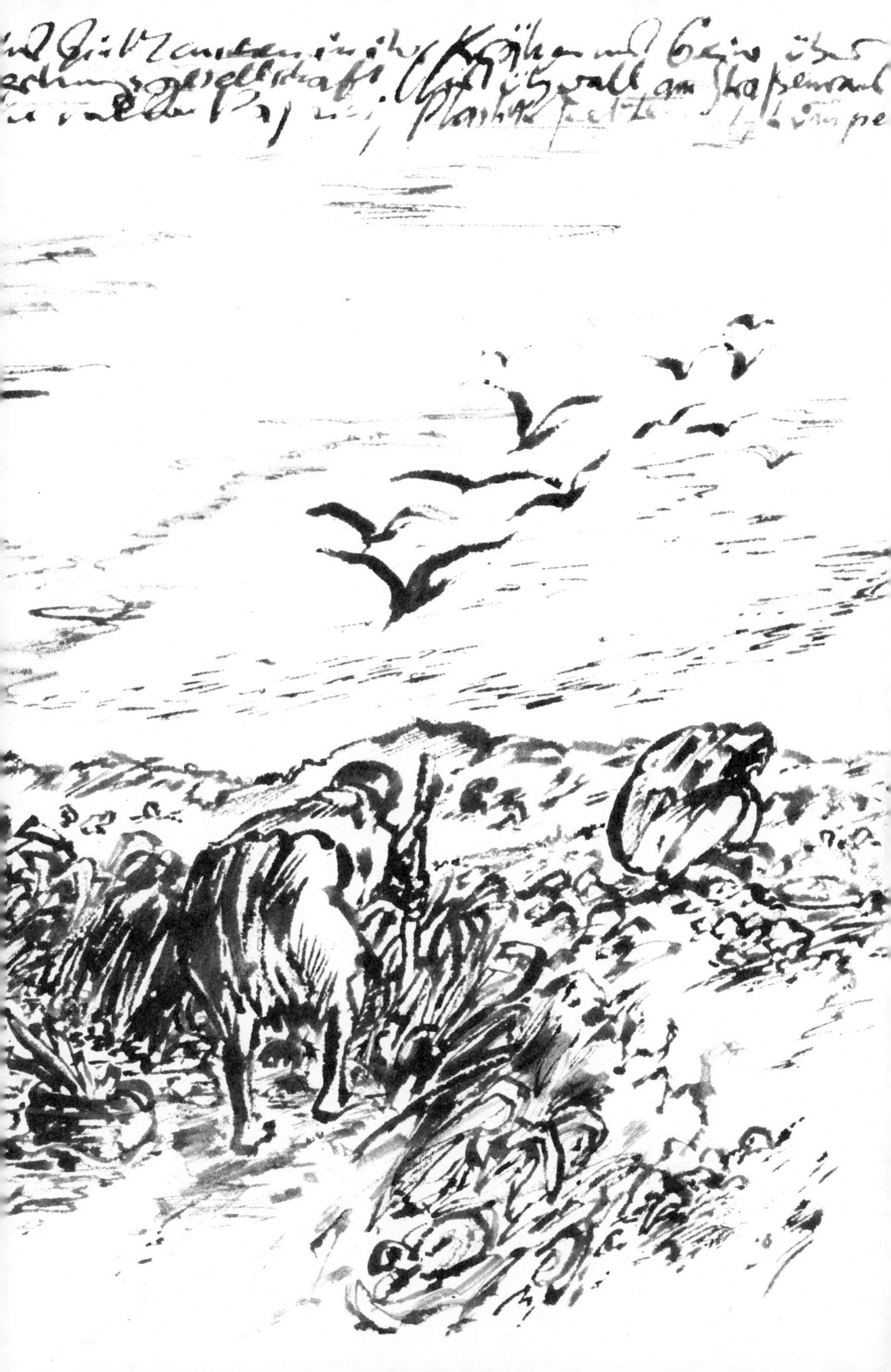
Krähen und Geier über
am Straßenrand

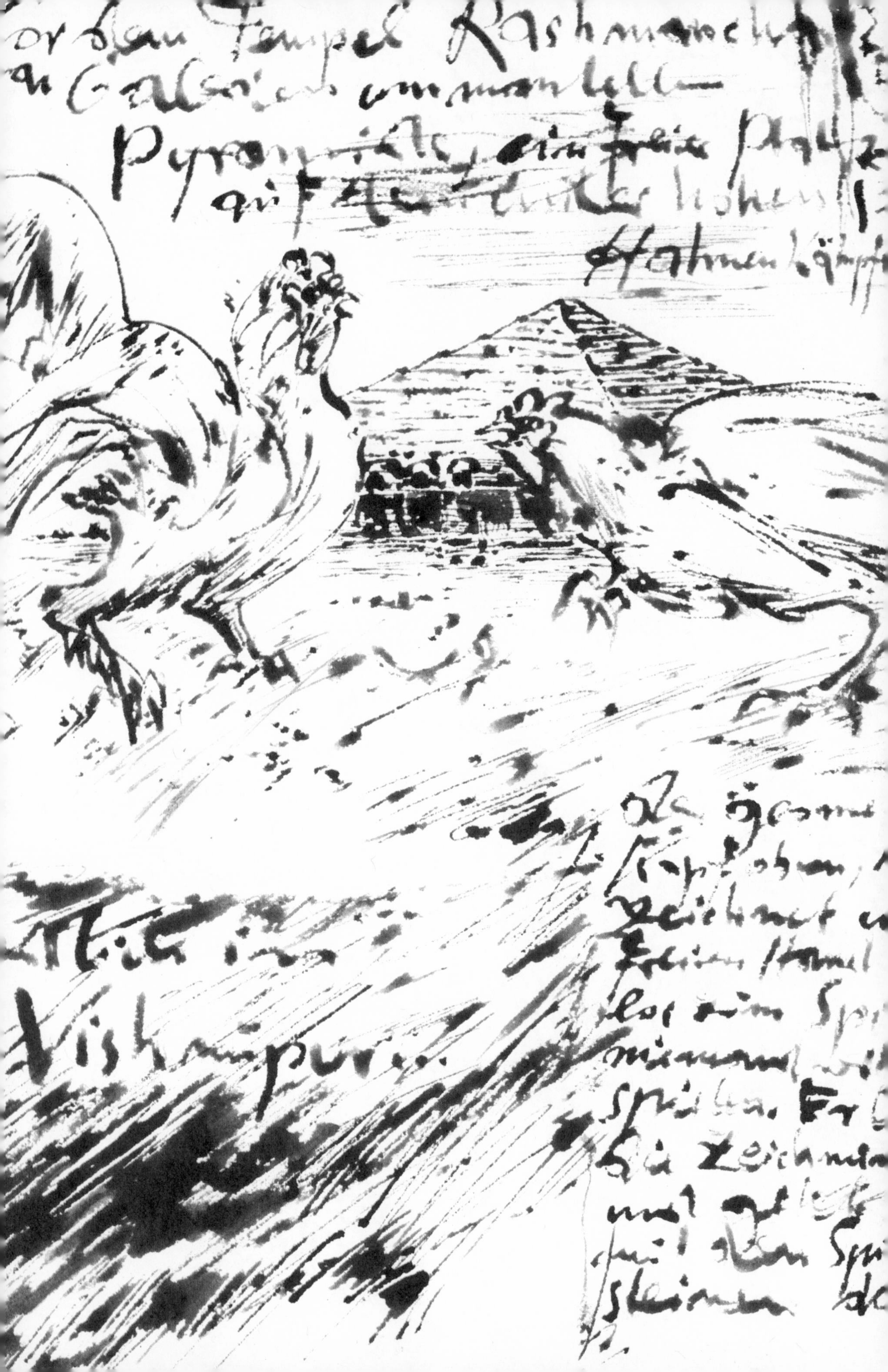
Mit in
Vishnupur.

Später Krähen drauf
die immer mehr Krähen
dem Himmel abziehen

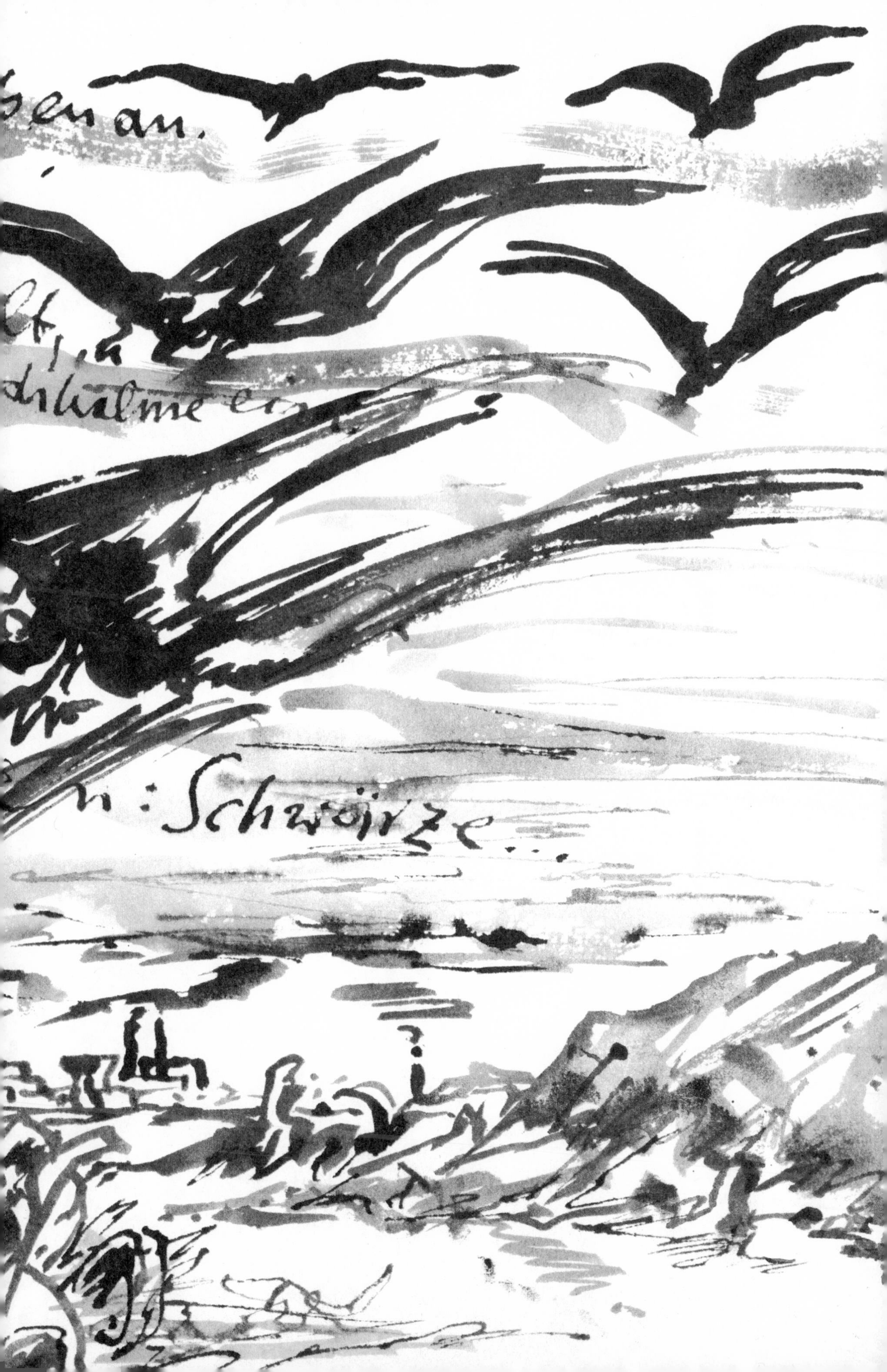

sen an.
n: Schwärze . . .

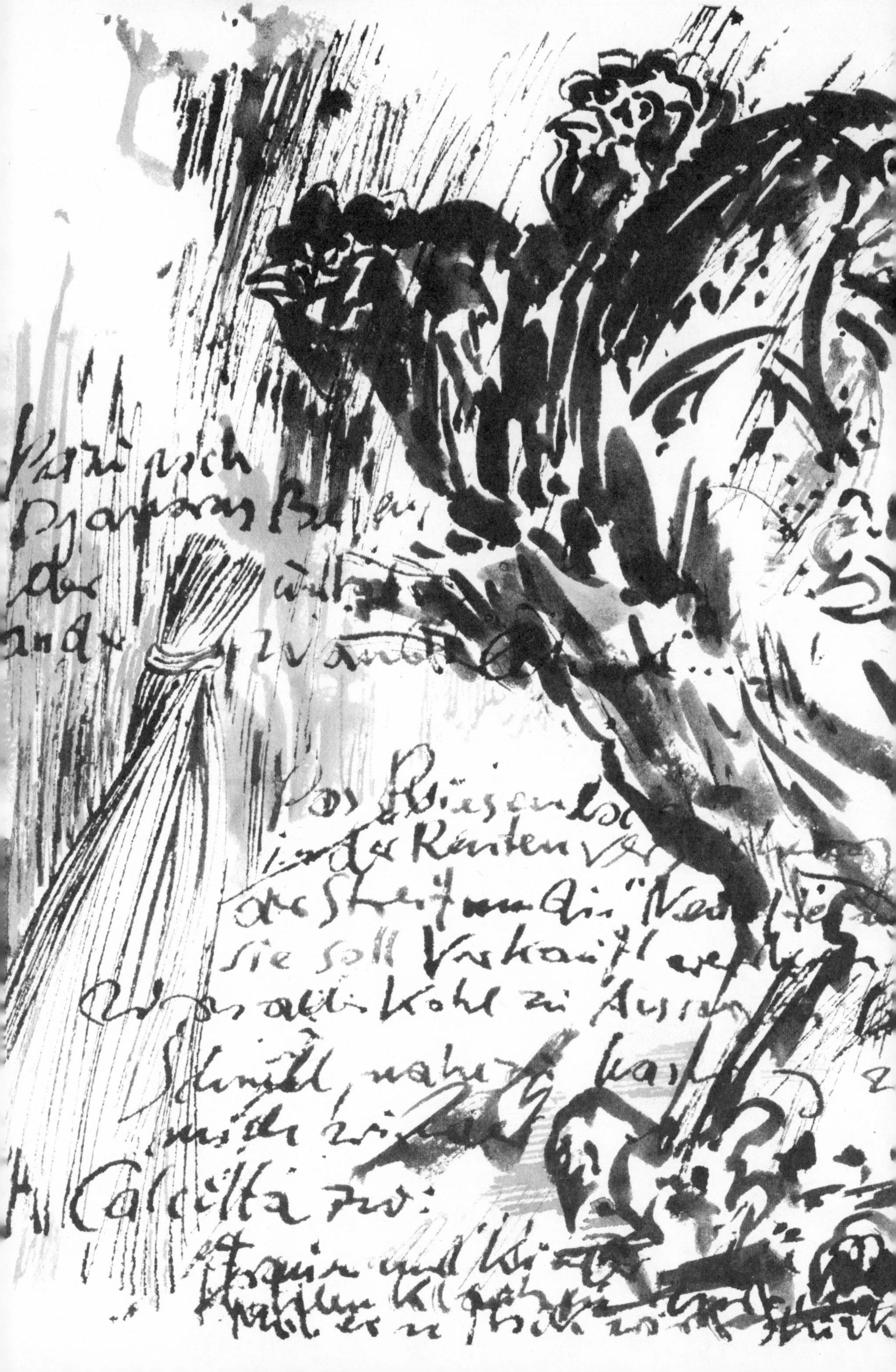

Gruppen,
Hunde dazwischen
heilig und fühllos
bewachen. Zwischen den
sehen wir einen wach liegend
unter der Bogenlampe

vom Platze der fünf mündenden Straße
dem Boxe, das Führerlein, in Bronze
Richtung Delhi reitet, im Mitternacht
Calcutta: da liegen sie, aus
pavement
Hauptstraße, nach Seald
weiter...
Schläfer
Kühe
Schla

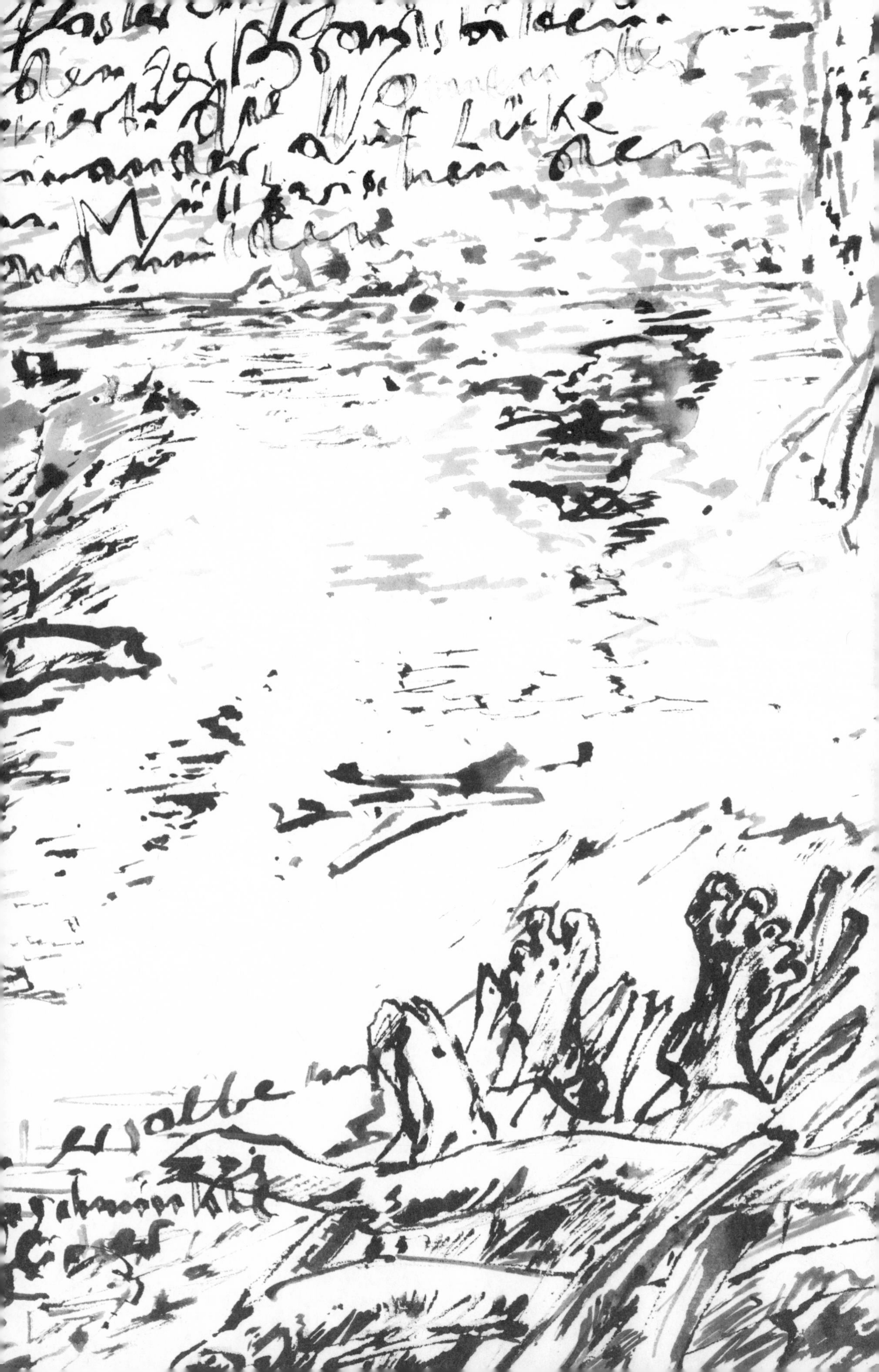
auf Lücke

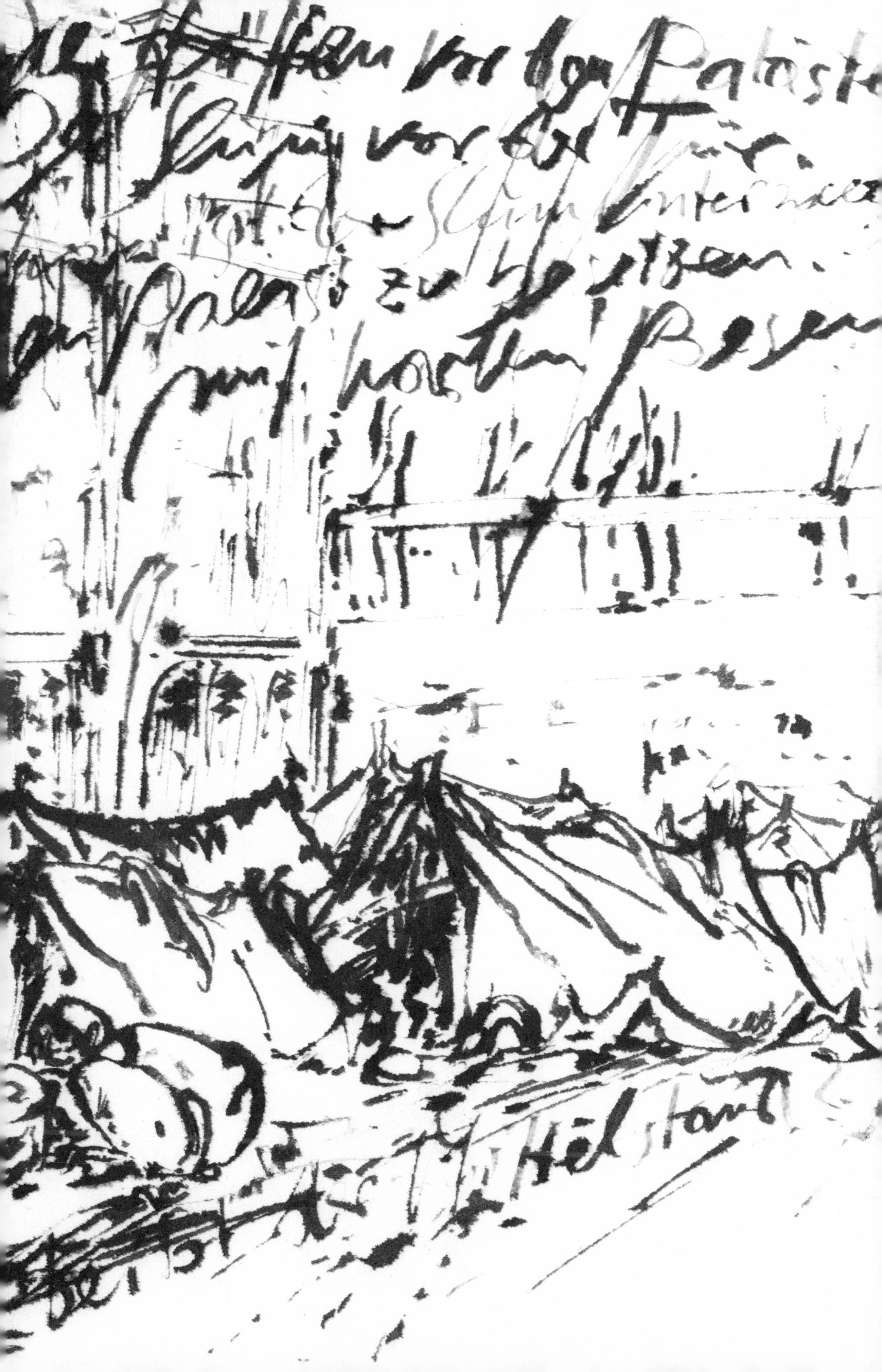
vor den Palästen
mit harten Besen

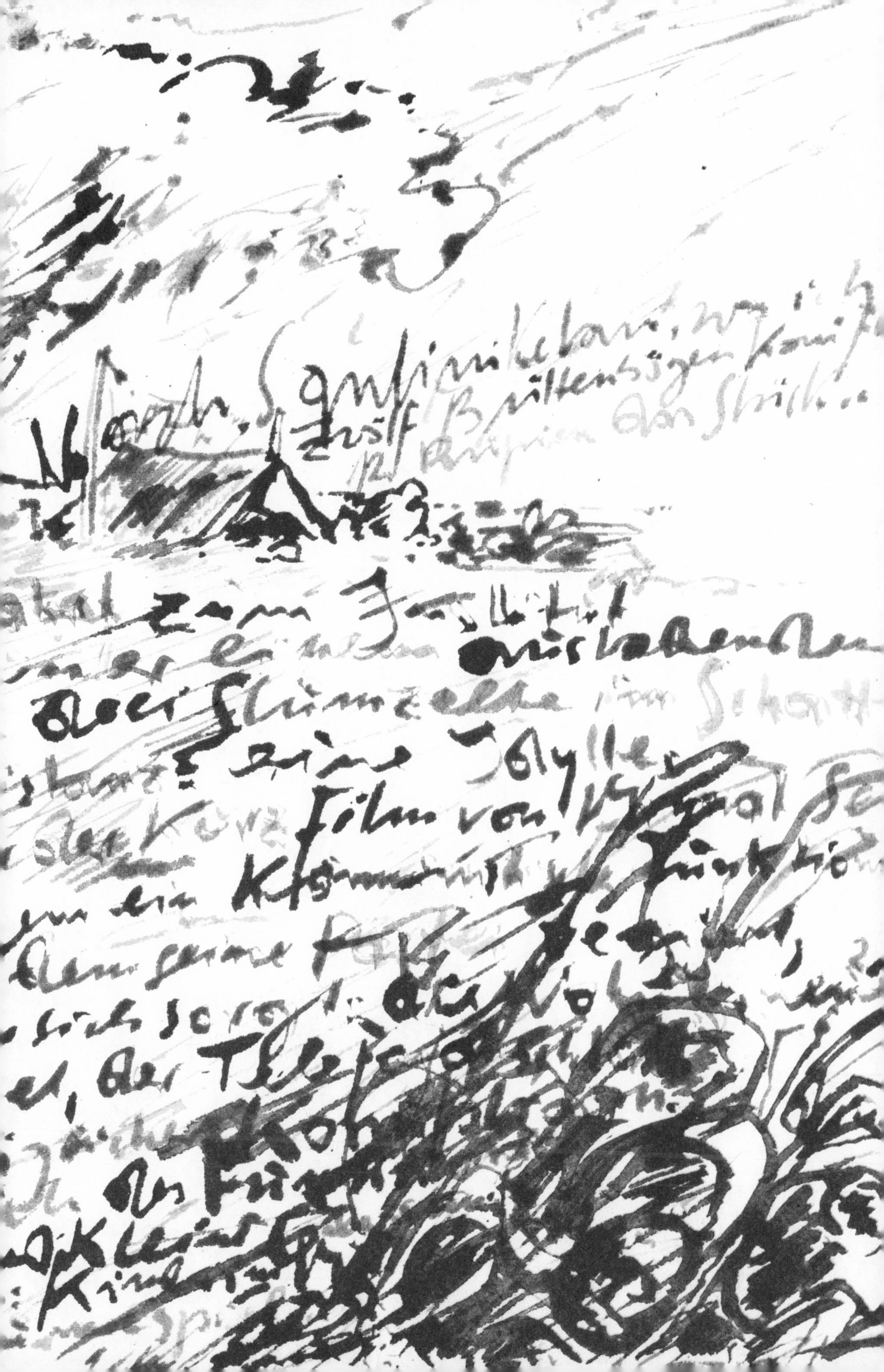
Film von

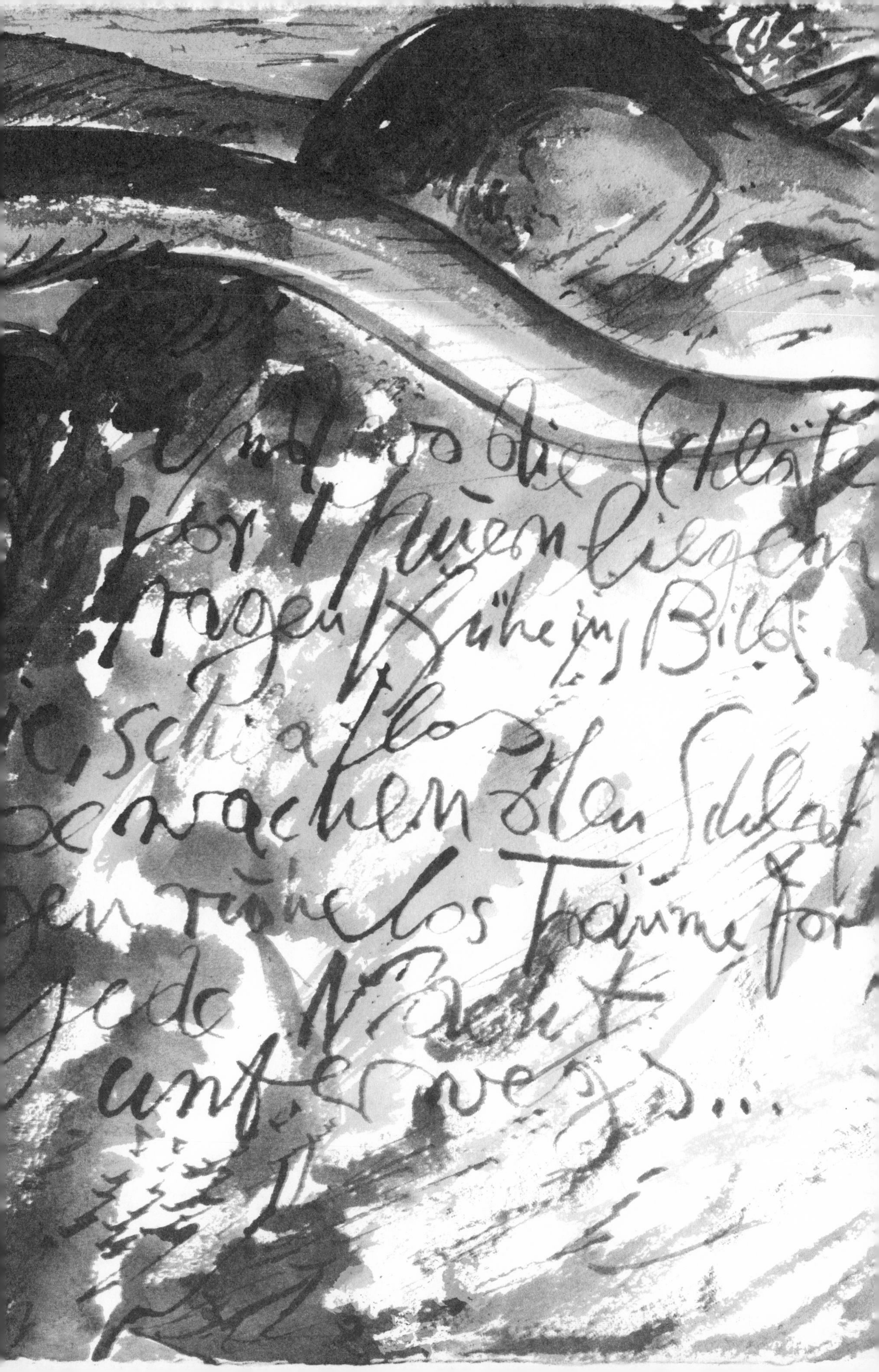
die Schläfe
liegen
ins Bild.
erwachen den Schlaf
Träume
jede Nacht
unterwegs...

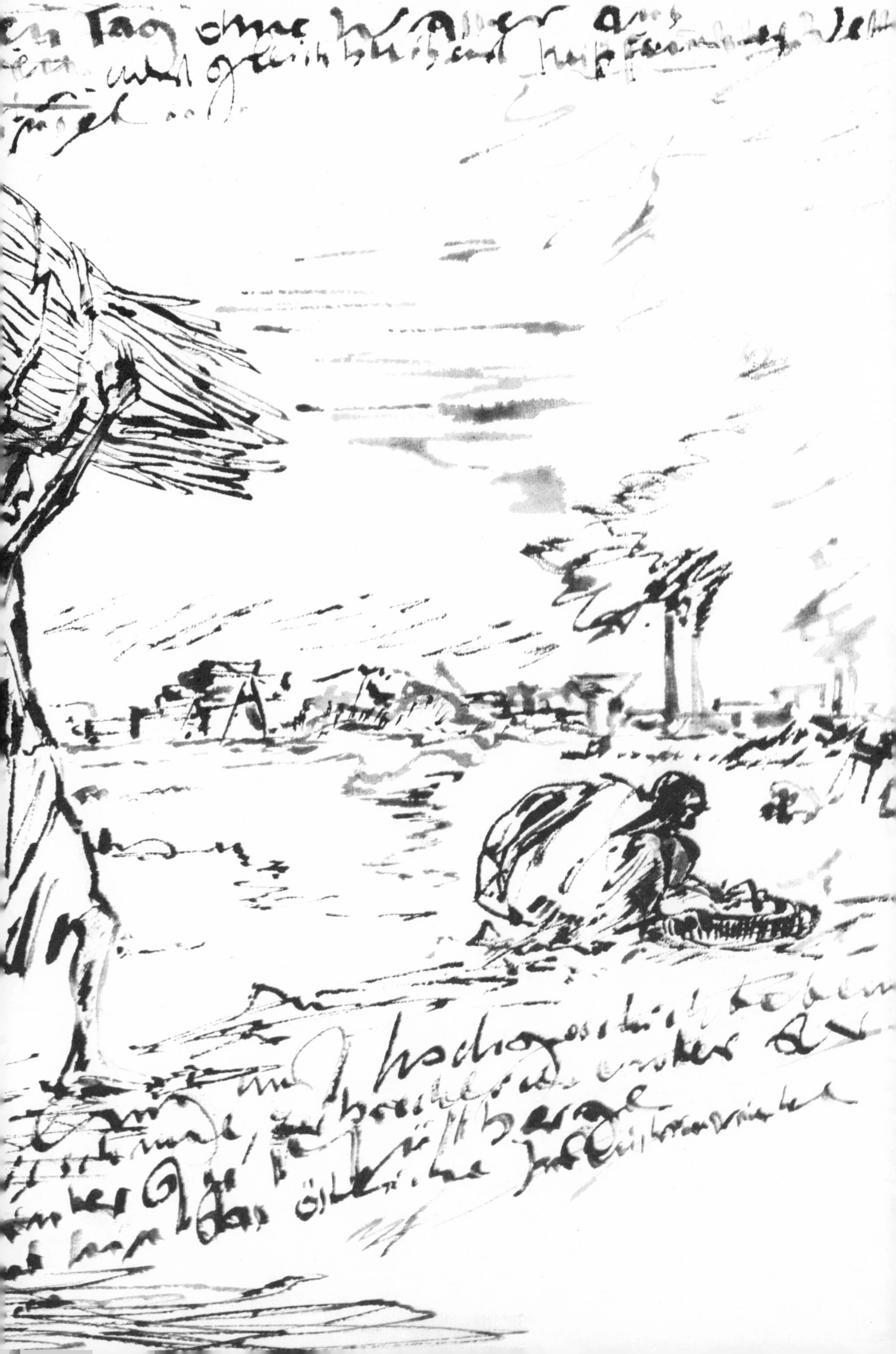

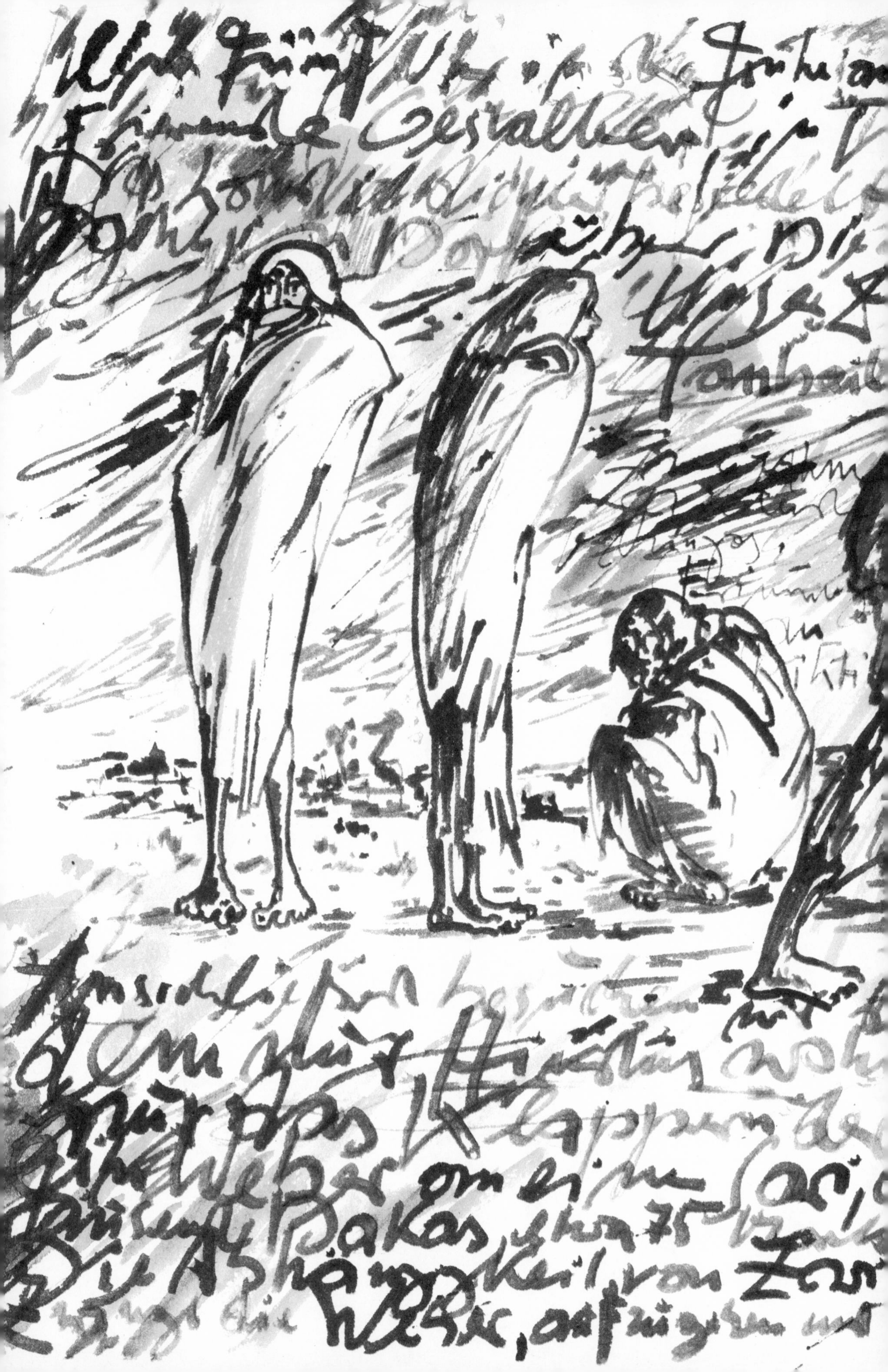

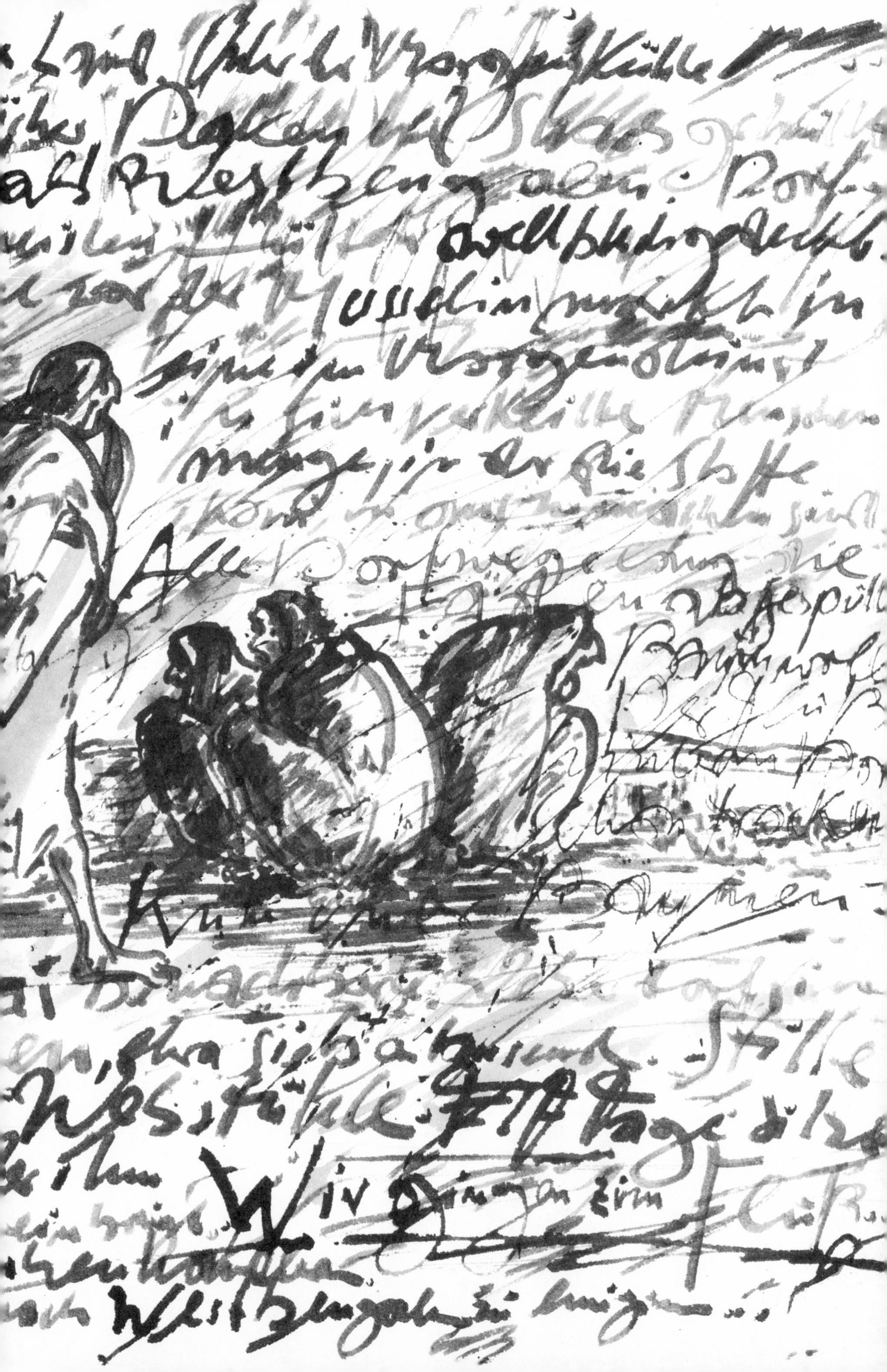

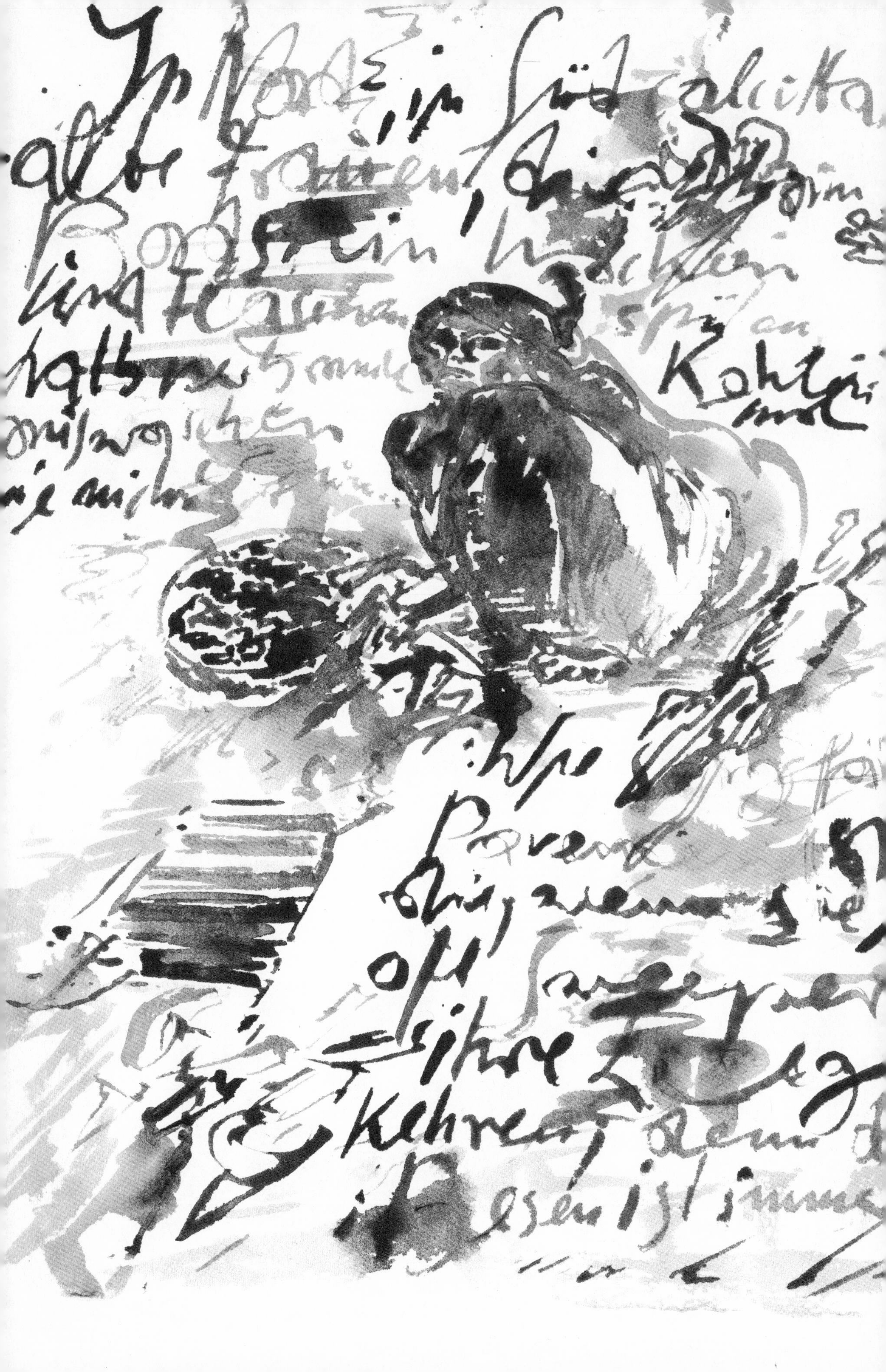

Kohle
oft
ihre
Kehren

Früher Vormittag:
Jetzt, nach elf
den Kühleren
die Schläfe
von Häus
die an

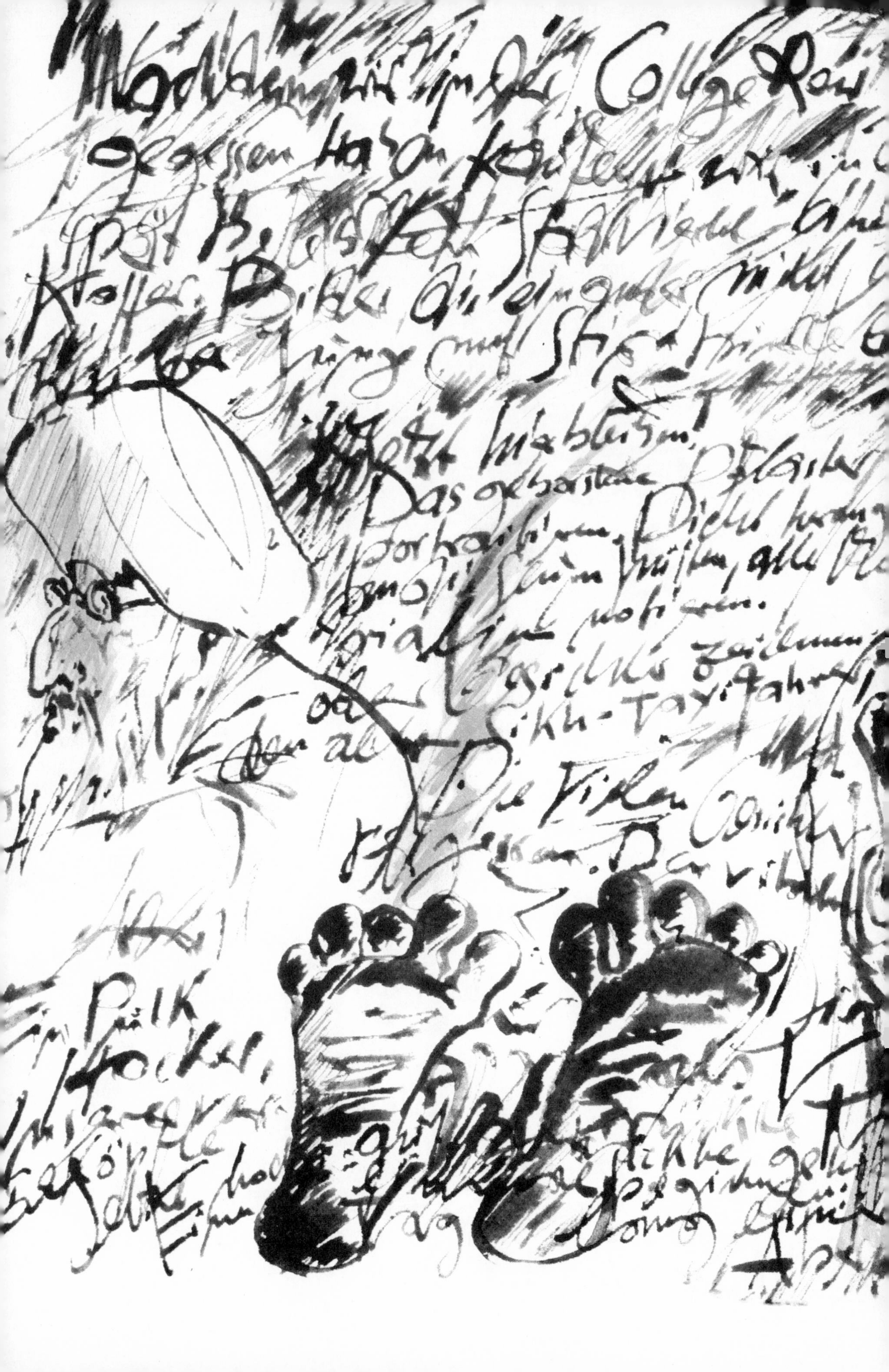

Show Your Tongue

1

Black, the goddess. Loosing themselves
black from trees, bats
black before the moon.

No more ah, alas, and every
angel is terrible. No thought
stands in line to close the pores.
It must be overabundance that another climate
has put on ice.
Here, they say at home, where no one
gets involved, nothing should be
extreme and only as compensation is terror
permitted. No sweat here!

All sluices open, it flows, drops
onto the sheet, makes
common cause with ink: I am
sopped through and set laughing by
sweat-driven words in tight ranks
encapsulated like us in our
commuter train to Ballygunge.

The, a, an get canceled.
The drift is general
when one licks another's sweat.
The old good grip gone, and the carpet too,
the heirloom underfoot, gone. We
have mislaid one another.

196

Silence, only the lip-smacking
of geckos, until the bus to Calcutta,
the resounding horn, the oncoming traffic,
and the neighbor's radio bawls love
like everywhere else.

This, every night. Yet today
the moon is full for an encore.

2

Their fall—people forgot to date it—
from whose hand, forgotten, and now
lying athwart, in rows, hemming the asphalt,
buried in shadow, they are pavement dwellers.

The past has passed: nobody
leaves a gap. Look
at them, death sleepers
they say, bellydown most of them,
real as photographs.

By edict abolish this sleep. Clean
it up, clear the view! No one
is allowed to die, at least not
in municipal public.

The statistics smile: everything is moving
and business as usual. Humans
in every direction multiply,
one behind the other, by
a factor of a thousand. So much
effort each day just to cross traffic,

jammed-wedged-finding space, losing
it again, wailing
horns and sirens as if
every moment must be denounced.

Rot blackens, green splits the walls
all the way up to the pomp, column-propped,
of overgrown capitals. Gap teeth
in the cornices. The colonial dream
dreams on, and at teatime, even now,
Lord Wellesley's ghost, stocking-footed, walks.

House-sized ads. World Bank plans
to save the city lie in a pile like
the garbage beside the road to Dum Dum,
another kind of daily inflation.
In notebook 9 Lichtenberg says
that in revolutionary times, "The sweepings
outside the city, in them you can read
what a city lacks, as a physician
reads stool and urine."

What is lacking? For dying,
nothing, but for life, naked
as the proverb has it, everything
except pure will.

3

A plummet of carrion crows. Black sheen
on stink. Beaked unrest
before a cohort of squatters in faded white
sitting away time on their heels,

motionless before the wall
occupied by parties before the election.

Who will accuse, where all confess,
who call out, where an echo
drowns each cry, and who
will hope, where on every wall
the hammer and sickle are peeling?

Tied into bundles, cheek by jowl, the future
in storage on cracked pavement. Step
over, leap the puddles left from the last
monsoon, seeking yourself, your bundle, one
laid among others. The loss
has left you speechless.

Yet you babble on about land reform, if
only it would come, and like remission
of sins, more water taps and ricksha licenses,
more words like renovation and powdered milk.

Humanity, they say, though at giveaway
prices, is in even greater supply, even
among Brahmans, and getting greater,
zero point six
percent, so that by the year 2000 . . .

The patience of poverty.
In rice fields, backs bent forever.
Amazing, man outoxens the oxen and still smiles.
The mystery of India, say the Indologists.

199

4

Roaring tigers that once in great
numbers roamed here now painted
on shop shutters with the goddess,
black, and her tongue, red.
Blow Horn! one truck requests another
in bright letters.

No sooner was the wheel invented and the road
built and a god put in charge of traffic, than
we had potholes and broken axles
and the belief, ever since, that from red light
to red light we are advancing.

The pavement paved with betel-juice snot.
It has the mange, pustules, festering boils.
Scratches itself raw. Scabby at the edges.
Poured gravel barf. Tar bandages.
Whatever the official patchers, between outages,
come up with.

Cracks run off on their own,
hoping to become crevasses.
Holes achieve craterhood!
Park Street or Gandhi Nehru Tagore Road,
not a street keeps its mouth shut,
they shout their ambition,
vomit back their medicine,
laugh themselves almost to death
at the increasing expense.

Under the sun, in the traffic, the blind man
jaywalks. Behold, a thought
makes the crossing safe, the surface flat.

What stinks to high heaven here are
sacrifices unaccepted, rejected, left lying.

5

Three vaccinations, and we are immune, not here,
escaped into comparisons. But were hit
in the gut, seeing, under the portal, an old cannon
caressed by children.

Far into the dome, the Queen
fills her museum. You see her
reading in the saddle, while her groom,
a Scotsman, holds the reins.
Victoria Memorial, the Empire's musty
back storeroom, built for a matron,
who, covered with bronze icing, clucks.

An age named for her. She loved her Indians,
especially the poor, Lord Curzon reports.

What would have happened had Hastings
not shot his rival, or, better yet, had Francis
wounded *him* in the side? But God,
biased since Cromwell, made Hastings hit
home, made India a crown jewel, let
Calcutta bloom into the mooncalf
of the sun never sets.

In coach and four, sleek arrogance infected
by the pox once drove lordly
down the Chowringhee. All that's left
are mildewed etchings colored by hand.

201

Gutters, fly shit, the climate actually
has always been ghastly, and in the cemeteries
freckle-faced lads, tender-aged, were laid
before they got to whiff powder.

Kipling, too, done in oils, farsighted
over the rim of his glasses, conquering provinces
to clothe them in khaki over the knee.

And what, we ask ourselves over tea,
would have happened had Bose,
photographed in civvies beside Hitler,
and in uniform on a reviewing stand in Singapore,
freed the subcontinent for Japan and turned
history east of the Suez upside down?

As we passed betel vendors, there were sheep
on the Maidan, an artillery range turned park.
Crows black in their wool. A man with drums
brought his monkey on a string. For us
the monkey danced Indian and rock 'n' roll.
A cloudburst, street flooding, haze over the city,
as in the paintings of Daniell, who in 1786
arrived with brushes, easel, and saw Venice.

6

Garbage, our own. Daily, provided a strike
doesn't put a stick in the wheel.
Dumpsters take the city's vomit
along the road to the airport, VIP Road,
creating landscape, changing the horizon daily,

and for many children the garbage is
foster mother, treasure quarry.

Everything is found, grabbed. Nothing,
from bottle cap to nail to vial to fixture to tube,
not even the refuse of the refuse is lost.

The stink, it comes from us,
our daily remains. Not just from the rich
does it dribble, the poor contribute too.
Mingled and sieved, it ferments
beneath the next monsoon. Our stink.

Yet, in excavations a thousand years from now
in alluvial flats from the last Great Flood,
the site of legendary Calcutta, nothing
will be found, no bottle cap, no nail, no vial,
no fixture or tube, not even
the refuse of the refuse, only silent garbage.

In the present garbage already
turning to humus, promising vegetables, we found
a school hidden in a shed, children
crouched over slates, practicing Bengali letters.
The exercise, written over and over,
in translation: Life is beautiful.

The vultures here know too much, know
what will be in the paper tomorrow.
Soon that computer, the one
the son of a sweeper,
say the vultures,
developed in his free time,
says the paper,

will regulate garbage collection. But
the stink won't be so easy to . . .

7

When it was over, the only survivors—
in one place only—were those who had learned
daily survival and kept their city, despite
its reputation for dying, alive and kicking.
The reward of the "bustling hell"
and "charming chaos,"
to quote the travel brochures
for that West Bengal metropolis.

And so for a while,
when Nothing was everywhere,
Calcutta celebrated its puja feasts and elected,
because politics too continued there, by a landslide,
what was known as the hammer and sickle
in former days.

Its citizens would have been able, strikes
and outages notwithstanding, to celebrate longer
had not—because of ice melting at the poles—
the floodwaters risen along the Hooghly.

We deeply regretted, said the She-rat,
who was conjured by my dream, this loss.
It was our city, too, you know,
that perished. There, for the crows and us,
was rice aplenty and garbage
like nowhere else. There we were
the darlings of the gods and men.

204

For the gods and for us, the death of the world
was a transition quick and painless.

I won't go on writing this, no,
good She-rat, no! Once again jute
will capture the market. Recently Birla
built a temple. It's the People's Front
at the next elections. And along
the patchwork streets people
have planted trees in pens of bast baskets,
trees, seedling upon seedling, trees.

Dragging itself on stump knees, too, hope lives.
Hordes swallowed and spewed by Howrah Station
cross the bridge trembling under its burden
to celebrate this day, certain of the next.
Durga Puja, Lakshmi Puja, then Kali Puja,
days that make everything cheaper,
remain promised to the gods.

Hope! Millions in credit are to fall upon
the city, and a state visit in bulletproof glass.
Even in the dark—even without moving fans—
poets sing undaunted: Tagore Tagore . . .
There is, good She-rat, no end in sight,
unless the end takes place before conception.

8

In yellowed white and milky brown, in hides
with the nap rubbed short, before train stations,
temples spilling garbage, or athwart

the circling traffic of rickshas
and no room for buses
public or private, solemnly strides,
as if through an undertow,
with right-of-way to passing
cardboard, bast, trash, the most recent rubbish—
bamboo. Bound to the wagon,
it points behind as it sways.

Cattle, horned patience
and the yoke still sacred. Godan,
bitter Prem Chand's (writing his fingers sore
in both Urdu and Hindi) exorbitant cow.
Cow that by the kilo and for Moslems only
flops beached on butchers' tables.
She lies, cud-chewing, in the path
of accelerated time, but herself is time,
gestator of calves. Gentle,
in this land where fear of touch is law,
gentle alone are the tongues
of cows and calves.

Burdens, no interest or interest on interest
or inherited debt. Lower than the low,
banned to burdens, allowed only to carry
water from putrid wells. Other burdens,
as if hovering, on the head, that no thought
cancels or dignifies. Banana leaves
lashed around bundles, under jute sacks billowed
to nightmare. He walks, stands, walks,
clearly a man:
forever stigmatized by his erect burdenlessness.

For pay, everywhere in the world
things are carried, but in Calcutta

we saw bearers of burdens
walk through the eye of the needle.

Too much, this is too much! Ease
the burden, the pulley of reason,
and hand over my bag. Look how it rises,
ahead of me, sure of its path through throngs,
while my knowledge rearranges concepts.
It's division of labor, I think as I pay.

Money stinks here, especially the smaller bills.
A clinging sourness. Counting out rupees, I
immediately want to wash my hands with soap.
Or a cow may come, sacred,
with its rough tongue.

When they lie down against ashen skies,
becoming soft mountains whose highest places fall
steeply to horns in front but gradually to the back,
they are a landscape herd, and the cow
foremost eats what the wind delivers,
yesterday's paper, with a small article
buried among other articles which tells
how in Bombay thousands of liters
of milk every day are mixed
with the Arabian Sea because the price
is too high and purchasing power too low,
though need is everywhere and on posters
big-eyed children . . .

Now the cows get up, the landscape retires.

9

Our plan, to flee. We withdraw,
a careful eye on the surging ocean,
from the turd-strewn beaches.
On temple roofs sacred monkeys tumble.
Above them, slit open by Jagannath's tower,
clouds bring rain. And more rain.

But the distant city, flooded
for days now because of a low
over the Bay of Bengal, though all the pumps,
seven operating out of eleven,
work in vain around the clock,
and because, too, exactly forty years ago,
as blood flowed around blood, corpses,
dismembered, were stuffed into drains
and ever since then the sewers back up.
Also, no cash flow, and plans remain plans,
so that what should be draining is rising.

Illustrious monsters of a history
whose dates are bouts of nausea.
Job Charnock and his son-in-law,
Bengali nabobs, the one named Siraj-ud-Daula,
who in two days in June of 1756
opened up the Black Hole
for the Brits who didn't make it
across the river, until from Madras
came Clive with his well-drilled sepoys
to wreak vengeance and get
swamp fever and silver.
Then the battle of Plassey,
as it was painted. Then,
not painted, a nationwide famine

208

that claimed every third person. And Divani,
the East India Company's double-entry books,
tax collectors pleasing to God. Then another
famine, millions dying as the Japanese
in Burma went from village to village
(Netaji, the little Führer, in their bag),
then the break: here East, there West,
murder before and after, refugees
swelling the city until in slow motion
the city
starts leaking refugees.

All this, gurgling in the drains,
rises up: heads round like coconuts,
bundled, sorted, believing
in one god, in many gods,
class enemies and Naxalites riddled with holes,
Kali at last, who measures our time:
nowadays, Last Days . . .

And yet the offer (as in legends)
of help from on high. Today he flew in,
the son of the murdering murdered widow,
bringing his central power with him, displaying it:
see, in low flight above the flooded villages,
rice fields, suburbs, slums,
and the camps of the six hundred thousand,
who, though without shacks, are nonetheless
voters.

But when the son of heaven landed,
old stern Basu, in white cotton
that purges (since Stalin) have washed,
who outlived all Indira's headcracking goondas,
did not smile, demanded kerosene.

Basu, literate like all Brahmans,
finds his Marx unhelpful, because
no passage in *Das Kapital* refers
to flooding shortly before religious festivals.

By the time we had the ocean
behind us and came from Howrah Station
across the bridge, the city was
cleaning, sweeping itself, dumping gravel
in all the holes. Columns of harijans
marched against the sludge, knee-deep.
Yet all the papers had predicted rain.

10

A downpour, reverberating thunder, like trucks
overloaded and lurching from pothole to pothole.

Annotated nature: rain, not a thread of it broken.
Lines and colons, verbatim speech:
tales of the gods assembled, authentic.
Krishna giggling, Ganesh, god with trunk,
whose name appears on bottles of mustard oil,
Durga, who for her feast lowers the prices.
Mantric drivel keyed to repetition. Sanskrit,
gods babbling in the tongue of priests.
Only the drums offer variation.

And yet aboard the 10:30 local from Baruipur
by way of Mullikpur Sonapur Garia Baghajatin
Jodabpur Dhakuria heading for Ballygunge
Station we saw, left, right,
fields submerged,

huts of clay and straw turned to islands.
Only the platforms above water,
the refuge of cows.
Wedged in the train car, we heard
a blind man sing.
Song, the privilege of the blind,
with hands open to make unmistakable
the demanding lament, to clear the way,
to hit nails on the head.
And, indeed, the blind man's song
didn't miss once.

This time the blind man was
a boy, his eyes milk.
With a brittle voice
he shoved through penned flesh
an aisle for himself.
His chant of need got off the 10:30 local
and visited, near Sonapur, more flood
upon the sinking huts.

Empty, however, the child's open hand.
As he stumbled among doves, we gave
quickly and in shame, anxious
not to do the
wrong thing.

But later over tea, language did treason,
the boy went wrong on me,
became a terrible angel.

11

Life comes to this sooner or later.
Bedded in branches, covered with sticks,
sticks weighed (as in a businessman's
Last Judgment), because wood costs,
reddish firewood felled in feverish sundarbans,
and the sticks must not be longer
than the cadaver.

At the burning ghats along the Ganges,
down to the banks of the Hooghly,
woodpiles smoldering, still damp
from water delivered again and again
like sudden birth (turning the city
into headlines around the world).
Reluctant still, that costly wood,
it needs to be coaxed with rice straw,
encouraged with words, revived.

Melted butter greases the dead.
Flowers on top, sweet of breath, cheerful.
Red paint on the soles of unaligned feet.
Leaves on dead eyes. But the phrases
we find obituarily handy—passed on,
sleeping the last sleep, went
to his reward—are unavailable.
The dead here are dead in earnest.

The wood takes them, the stump-toothed
fire gnaws through.
Renewed, elsewhere, perhaps, the soul.
Ashes and charred scraps belong to the river,
to which everything is added: excrement,

petals, chemicals, the bathers' fragile nakedness,
the sweat of faded cloth.

But today Durga and Lakshmi and company
are carted with hoopla and rat-a-tat
to the Hooghly.
The feast is over. For seven days
the gods have visited.
Straw puppets, to which clay (dried and lacquered)
lends the aspect of flesh.
Displayed: the lion and hoot owl,
the rat, peacock, and swan. And on ten arms
glistening power, so that good
may defeat evil, and similar nonsense.

In every slum even the poorest
of the poor raise high their altar,
Veteran Marxists drive six thousand beggars
out of town, out of sight, for as long
as divinity holds its feast.

Prayers and priests, as everywhere, have
their price. The price is fear. We could do
with a little anger.

12

Saw three brooms, no, four dancing
in the empty room. Or a single broom,
stiff straws bound together, danced
the rooms empty and pointed,
on its rounds, to scene after scene,

213

while outside the Untouchable ran off,
laughing: Clean up your own mess!

Saw, overturned, the belly of the city.
Monuments inverted. Saw the crawlers
set on their feet. The clean ones
and their well-bred daughters consigned
to garbage and rags and no longer giggling.
Saw columns of Brahmans cleaning latrines.
The heroes of amorous Hindi films banished
from the screen and driven into life,
that belched on them, taught them
to shit watery shit under the sun.
Saw big money go begging for tiny coins.

Patience at an end, furious,
on her pile of coconuts mixed with heads,
the heads of Hindus and Moslems
sliced whistle-clean
as blond-eyelashed British eyes looked on,
the goddess, black on Siva's pink belly,
squats unblinking.

Kali Puja announced, I saw Calcutta
descend on us. Three thousand slums,
usually rapt in themselves, crouched low
by walls or sewer water, now all
ran out, rampant, beneath the new moon,
the night and the goddess on their side.

Saw, in the holes of uncountable mouths,
the lacquered tongue of black Kali
flutter red. Heard her smack her lips:
I, numberless, from all the gutters
and drowned cellars, I,

set free, sickle-sharp I.
I show my tongue, I cross banks,
I abolish borders.
I make
an end.

They left (he and she), though the newspaper
kept arriving, with reports of kerosene
shortages, hockey goals, and Gurkha land,
and of waters that were gradually,
in Midnapore, gradually receding.

(The festival in honor of the black divinity,
said the *Telegraph*, took place
without incident.)

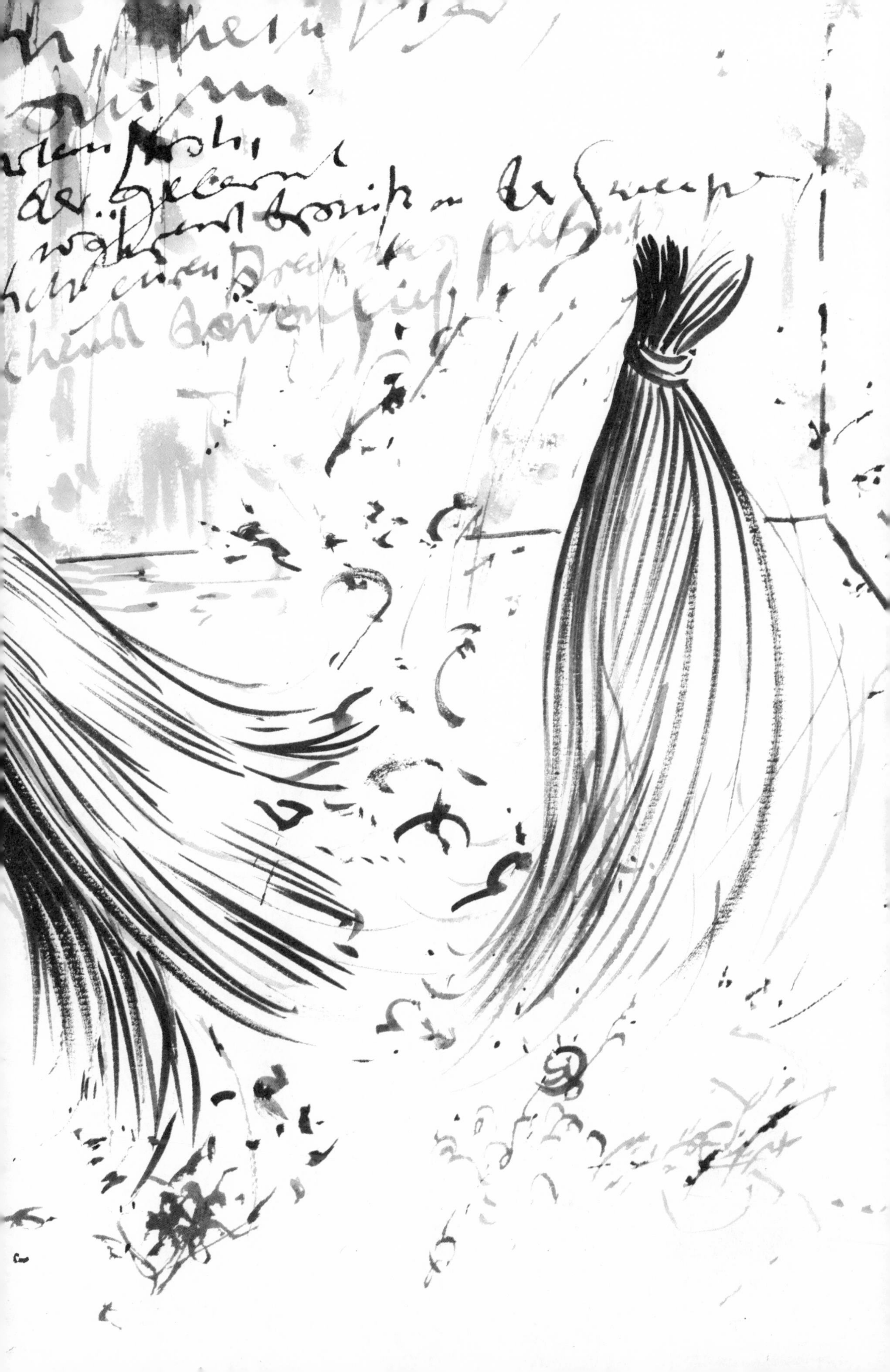

Postscript

Theodor Fontane (1819–1898) and his wife, Emilie, were descended from French Huguenots who emigrated to Prussia to escape religious persecution. Though trained as an apothecary, Fontane turned to literature. In 1844 he visited England, and later lived and worked there (1855–1859) as a journalist, partially with a political mission. He began his literary career writing ballads, and he also translated the ballads of England and Scotland. His abiding fame, however, rests with his novels, widely read and admired to this day for their elegance of style and psychological finesse.

*

George Christoph Lichtenberg (1742–1799), a German physicist and satirist, was renowned for his aphorisms that ridiculed the pseudosciences of his day.

*

In Grass's play *The Plebeians Rehearse the Uprising*, a rehearsal of Shakespeare's *Coriolanus*, under the direction of Bertolt Brecht, is juxtaposed with the bloody suppression of the workers' uprising in East Berlin, June 17, 1953.

Contents

Will need lots of black ink

Feet dumped out, deployed

For the broom is always with them

And everywhere cows are part of the
scene

Silence, only the tapping of the
stonemasons

A single mountain with a face

Weighed down with stones

Tobacco workers, still dusty

The old Sikh, the many faces

Wrapped in cloths and blankets

Show Your Tongue   196

Saw three brooms, no, four

Under the access bridge

A flock of crows

Postscript   222